Zora Neale Hurston

Titles in the series Critical Lives present the work of leading cultural figures of the modern period. Each book explores the life of the artist, writer, philosopher or architect in question and relates it to their major works.

In the same series

Zora Neale Hurston

Cheryl R. Hopson

REAKTION BOOKS

For my students, mentors and family

Published by Reaktion Books Ltd
Unit 32, Waterside
44–48 Wharf Road
London N1 7UX, UK
www.reaktionbooks.co.uk

First published 2024
Copyright © Cheryl R. Hopson 2024

Printed and bound in Great Britain by Bell & Bain, Glasgow

A catalogue record for this book is available from the British Library

ISBN 978 1 78914 795 7

Contents

Zora Neale Hurston with her purse and hat in hand. In her overcoat, she is clearly a woman on a mission.

Introduction

Just squat down awhile and after that things begin to happen.[1]

In 1917, in a letter to William Pickens, dean of Morgan Academy in Baltimore, Maryland (a secondary school that would later become Morgan State University), Zora Neale Hurston, then a student at the academy, wrote: 'I want to *know* you and Mrs Pickens . . . I want to reverse the usual process, & know the writing by the writer.'[2] Pickens was an accomplished writer whose books included *Abraham Lincoln, Man and Statesman* (1910), *The Heir to Slaves* (1911) and *Bursting Bonds* (1923), the last two being autobiographies.

In this letter, Hurston establishes what I suggest is a key aspect of her process as a writer: she founded and maintained relationships via letter writing with powerful and influential men and women, through whom she became able to access some measure of power and influence for herself in the fields of literature, linguistics, folklore and anthropology – and, significantly, education and travel. This desire to know and be known, here via the discursive mode of the epistle, is a strategy Hurston employs to instil herself in the lives and consciousness of individuals with whom she may be able to partner, and to achieve her desired goal of an education and in effect a greater, more expansive life. In the case of Pickens, Hurston seems to have sought, and won in some measure, access to a larger community of influential Black and white elite figures for whom she sometimes did paid domestic work to help supplement her education while at Morgan Academy. It is by way of the epistle that Hurston made herself known as a student at the academy to the dean of the school.

She knew how to compel an audience through writing. Hurston was as much a pragmatist as she was a diviner. Despite common considerations of her as frivolous and careless with her life (and work), she was anything but. Hers were generally decided-upon moves.

In asking to ingratiate herself into Pickens's life and that of his wife, Hurston was, by her own admission, both 'pushing the limits of decorum' and stretching her 'impertinen[ce]'. However, she ends her letter with 'Yours Respectfully', a return to formality and a reestablishment of her understanding of her place in relation to the dean, the dictates of Morgan Academy decorum and the larger Black and white intellectual and elite classes she was now among.

Most compellingly, Hurston's wish to pry into the Pickenses' life showcases an early interest held by the future novelist, folklorist and anthropologist to study as well as write about the lives and ways of Black Americans. Less than a decade later, in a letter of 12 May 1925 to Annie Nathan Meyer, a writer, educator and co-founder of Barnard College in New York City (and Hurston's future benefactor), Hurston writes of 'striving desperately for a toe-hold on the world'.[3] She continues, 'It is a mighty cold comfort to do things if nobody cares whether you succeed or not,' and confides further: 'It is terribly delightful to me to have some one fearing with me and hoping for me, let alone working to make some of my dreams come true.'[4] Most telling in this letter is the work Hurston does to persuade Meyer that she is not haughty, which is to say, above her station in a society stratified by class, sexism, capitalism and racist Jim Crow laws.

What Hurston's 1917 letter to Pickens and her 1925 letter to Meyer – both writer-educators – reveal are relational dynamics influenced by power differentials as well as by differences of race, sex, gender, class and region. Significantly for Hurston, and as these letters show, hindrances to access – a prerequisite of which was whiteness or maleness – required negotiation. In both letters, Hurston was writing as a student to individuals with the means and resources to help her achieve her goal of higher education. Hurston would continue on from Morgan Academy to Howard University in

A younger Zora with a friend, either at Morgan Academy or Howard University. Hurston was upfront about the fact that even though her Black women classmates sometimes mocked her for her poverty, they were also quick to lend her items from their own closets to wear when the occasion necessitated.

Washington, DC, eventually matriculating at Barnard College with the financial backing of Meyer.

At both Morgan Academy and Howard, Hurston studied literature and drama and began the serious practice of writing. At Barnard, she received a degree in the discipline of anthropology. bell hooks writes, 'Anthropology, once defined as the "study of alien beings," captured the imagination of Zora Neale Hurston when she was seeking a course of academic study that would be compatible with her longing to write.'[5] Hurston's letters reflect, as do her later non-fiction and fiction writings, that she was already straddling the world of the researcher and the artist. Her letters reveal a compelling interlocutor and a gifted writer. Hurston was charming – as these correspondences and all of her letters collected in Carla Kaplan's *A Life in Letters* (2002) as well as in Hurston's archives at the University of Florida, Gainesville, show. Hurston's charm, perhaps a gift from her handsome and charismatic father, Reverend John Cornelius Hurston, would come in handy in Washington, DC,

Hurston, *c.* 1927, possibly during her time as an undergraduate – and the first African American student – at Barnard College in New York.

when she met with resistance, which Hurston did often in her life and work. It would also be useful when she met with success and acclaim, which she also did, and also often.

The novelist, anthropologist and folklorist Zora Neale Hurston (1891–1960) crafted a career that spanned the 1920s into the 1950s, a period of time in the United States that includes the Harlem Renaissance, the interwar decades and the rise of literary modernism in U.S. and Black American literature and culture. Hurston was among the first freeborn generation of African Americans on her father's side, and the second generation of freeborn African Americans on her mother's side. Here I am – as Hurston herself complained in her essay 'How It Feels to Be Colored Me' (1928) – reminding readers that Hurston was the daughter

Hurston, *c.* 1919–23, during her time at Howard University. Well dressed, with perfect hair untouched by the hat she holds in her hands, Hurston looks almost pensive as she stares into the camera.

and granddaughter of formerly enslaved people. I do so because this herstory (a neologism coined in 1968 by the U.S. feminist Robin Morgan to mean history told from a woman's or feminist perspective), which doubles as a narrative of U.S. and Black history, had a direct influence on Hurston's lived reality as well as on her work. Hurston wrote and conducted research in imagined scenarios as well as theorized from the perspective of a Black woman, and in particular from the perspective of a Black woman from the American South. Hurston's personal history and herstory matter to any critical understanding and consideration of her professional life, creative output and legacy.

As a girl and woman, if not always as a writer, Hurston understood her value early on in life. She understood that her material poverty did not equate to any kind of spiritual or personal poverty. This firm foundation of self-knowledge and self-worth was the stuff on which Hurston would build herself up from the frontier that was Eatonville, Florida, where she grew up, and out of the squalor in which she lived after her mother died in 1904. Even today, the idea of a professional, autonomous Black woman – and one with a platform – ruffles feathers. Imagine the response of women and men, Black or white and across classes and caste, to Hurston as a Barnard-educated anthropologist conducting fieldwork independently, using her own money and means, in the U.S. South, the Bahamas, Haiti and Honduras from the late 1920s to the 1940s. Hurston walked many a tightrope with friends, publishers and benefactors and drew on the epistle as her primary way of communicating, since it was cheaper than the telephone, newly in use, or even a telegram. Hurston met and repudiated powerful resisting forces to establish herself as a thinker, a scholar and an authority on Black life, art and culture.

Hurston had no models. She was not apolitical but neither was she ever overtly political in her creative work. She primarily wrote about love affairs between pretty Southern Black American characters adept at wordplay and philandering. Hurston rejected victimhood of any kind, but especially the sort that focused on her being a Black woman from a shifting class background whose personal history included the former enslavement of members of her immediate family. Hurston made every attempt to 'jump at the sun', a commandment of her beloved mother, Lucy Ann Potts Hurston, and in so doing she lived an inspiring, and inspired, life.

1

Childhood

Zora Lee (Neale) Hurston was born on 7 January 1891 in Notasulga, Macon County, Alabama, though she would forever give her birth state as Florida and her home town as Eatonville, the first incorporated all-Black town in the United States.[1] The fifth of her parents' eight children, and their second and youngest daughter, Hurston's birth preceded by one year her family's relocation from Notasulga to Eatonville. Like most other migrants, the Hurston family left Alabama in search of greater economic and life opportunities. Instead of migrating north, as did many African Americans from the close of the nineteenth century into the first half of the twentieth century, Hurston's parents headed southeast to the area whose name was on everyone's tongue, the all-Black town of Eatonville, where there was opportunity and work, and no white folks lording it over others.

At the time of Hurston's birth, her mother, Lucy, was 26 years old, and her father, John Cornelius Hurston, was 30. Lucy would go on to give birth to three more children, all boys, after Zora. Within five years of the family's relocation to Eatonville, Hurston's parents owned 2 hectares (5 ac) of land and a five-bedroom house that John himself built, most likely with help from his older sons. Hurston's parents had been sharecroppers in Alabama, which is to say only one foot beyond economic slavery; their economic lot in life seems to have improved in leaps and bounds upon their relocation to Eatonville.

The Hurston scholars Ann R. Morris and Margaret M. Dunn provide insight into the frontier-like scene of Eatonville during the author's childhood, writing, 'it was not unusual for the young Hurston to see alligators raiding hog pens, wildcats fighting yard dogs, and huge rattlesnakes lying across doorsteps. Nearby she could pick wild violets in the woods or play beneath the moss-draped oaks.'[2] They continue, 'On summer evenings [Hurston] could hear the mockingbirds singing all night in the orange trees while alligators bellowed in the nearby Lake Belle.'[3] As her writing reflects, Hurston absorbed and was inspired by Florida's flora and fauna, as well as by her adopted state's human inhabitants. What John and Lucy Hurston perhaps hoped for and anticipated in moving their family from their homestead of Alabama to the frontier that was Eatonville (then a town of only 125 residents) was a way of giving themselves and their children a community free of white Americans, a home in which they could grow and thrive, and do so among people with whom they shared a history and traditions.

Eatonville and its Black inhabitants were for Hurston a linguistic, experiential and creative treasure trove that was central to her own unique, early twentieth-century Black arts and Black aesthetics. If others struggled to see that Hurston was 'drenched in light', to invoke the title of one of her earliest published short stories,[4] her mother Lucy did not struggle and instead welcomed and fostered a space for Zora's difference, that is, her spirit of curiosity, storytelling and daydreaming, within the family. However, when Hurston was just thirteen years old, her mother died. Lucy passed away on 18 September 1904 at the age of 39, leaving behind eight children between the ages of 5 and 21. Lucy also left behind a widowed husband and father, who would soon marry a woman six years Hurston's senior and abandon his responsibilities towards his children, perhaps especially towards his daughters, Zora and her older sister, Sarah.

In October, just a few short weeks after her beloved mother's death, Hurston was sent away by her father to attend Bible school in Jacksonville, Florida. In her autobiography *Dust Tracks on a Road* (1942), Hurston writes of her time at the school: 'I worshipped two of my teachers and loved gingersnaps with cheese, and sour pickles.

But I was deprived of the loving pine, the lakes [of Eatonville], the wild violets in the woods and the animals I used to know.'[5] Reflecting on what she was missing, she wrote, 'No more holding down first base on the team with my brothers and friends. Just a jagged hole where my home used to be.'[6] Hurston mourned the loss of her mother and the dispersing of her family, but she would soon come to mourn for another reason: her father's neglect and abandonment of her. When John stopped paying Zora's tuition, she was put to work in the school's kitchen and laundry and worked Saturdays on campus cleaning stairs to cover her room and board. At the close of the school year, John did not send for his youngest daughter and instead insisted that the school, a Christian academy, keep her.

What must Zora Neale Hurston, motherless and away from home at age thirteen, have felt upon learning from school officials that her father did not want her? It is heartbreaking to imagine. Valerie Boyd's *Wrapped in Rainbows: The Life of Zora Neale Hurston* (2003) details the moment and explains that the academy's administrator eventually loaned her the fare to return home to Eatonville, albeit with the proviso that her father must repay the money. Boyd writes that Hurston was told that the school 'had no place' for her 'by the second in command, the same sharp-tongued administrator who had yelled Zora's financial distress out the window for all her classmates to hear', and who later, in a moment of softness, loaned Hurston the boat fare to return home to Eatonville.[7] What did Hurston learn about family and educational institutions in this moment? What did she glean about her relationship with her father? Why was the attempt at humiliation by a school administrator, at a time of crisis for Hurston, necessary or even accepted? Was this the moment, in 1905, when Hurston lost any real relationship with or connection to religion beyond the sense of it as a story and a wish? And what did John Hurston's turning away do to young Zora's spirit, to her heart, to her sense of confidence in, if nothing else, her father and her family?

Alone and in the new, inhospitable environment of Jim Crow Jacksonville, where was young Hurston to put her feelings? The reverberations of John's parental and paternal desertion must surely have had implications for not only the way Hurston experienced, imagined and engaged with men but the way she characterized Black American men in her fiction. We may consider, for example, Hurston's depiction of the character John Pearson in her first novel, *Jonah's Gourd Vine* (1934), a work that centres the life experiences of a Black itinerant preacher and that is loosely based on the life and marriage of Hurston's parents. In the novel, John Pearson is a philandering, charismatic, smart and yet befuddled husband, father and Baptist minister who barely gives a thought to his children. We may also consider Hurston's construction of Janie Crawford's white father in her second novel, *Their Eyes Were Watching God* (1937), a schoolteacher who imprisons, rapes and abandons Janie's Black mother, Leafy, without penalty, and whom Janie never meets.

In 1896, *Plessy v. Ferguson*, a ruling by the u.s. Supreme Court, sanctioned white apartheid in the form of Jim Crow law and rendered Black Americans as second-class citizens within the nation. This legal ruling henceforth altered the landscape of the postbellum nation for Black and white Americans alike. Hurston at the time was five years old, ensconced in the all-Black town of Eatonville. By then, Hurston was already 'everybody's Zora', quick-witted and considered too brazen for her own good.[8] In these surrounds, it would be years before she felt the proverbial wolf at the door that was Jim Crow.

Hurston was born 26 years after the dissolution of 240 years of legal, race-based slavery in the United States. She was the daughter of a man who himself was born into slavery and the granddaughter of a maternal grandmother who lived much of her life under slavery. For most of the nation's history, not only was a portion of the u.s. population legally enslaved, and through which illiteracy was legally enforced, but another portion – that is, its largely white population – imposed de facto and de jure laws intended to keep Black Americans in slavery in perpetuity. In doing so, the white population benefited economically, socially, politically, legally, culturally, educationally and in other ways; the denial of such benefits to enslaved and free African Americans is felt to this day, and these deficits informed the lives of Hurston's research subjects and Black folk characters. Hurston was born following Reconstruction in the u.s. South, which began in 1865 and ended in 1877. By the time of her birth in 1891, any progress won by African Americans in freedom was quickly being undercut or outright obliterated, and Hurston was brought up in a postbellum national landscape that legitimized segregation laws. In 1954, *Brown v. Board of Education* overturned *Plessy v. Ferguson*, rendering legal segregation unconstitutional.

For almost the entirety of her life – right until her 63rd year – Hurston made a living for herself as a writer and researcher, in the context of a race-, class- and gender-stratified, oppressive society that privileged whiteness, maleness and the lawful use of force and power. In *The African-American Odyssey* (2000), the historians Darlene Clark Hine, William Hine and Stanley Harrold provide insight into some of the material and psychological ramifications of Jim Crow laws for African Americans. In particular, they detail aspects of what they call the 'racial etiquette' dictating interactions between Black and white Americans during the decades following Reconstruction, and leading up to the *Brown v. Board of Education* decision.[9] 'Black and white people', they assert, 'did not shake hands. Black people did not look white people in the eyes.' Instead, Black people 'were supposed to stare at the ground when addressing white men and women'.[10] In addition, Black 'men removed their hats in the presence of white people,' but white men 'did not remove their hats in a black home or in the presence of a black woman'. They continue:

> Black people went to the back door, not the front door, of a white house. A black man or boy was never to look at a white woman . . . in the face, white customers were always served first, even if a black customer had been the first to arrive . . . Black women could not try on clothing in white businesses . . . White people did not use titles of respect – Mr, Mrs, Miss – when addressing black adults [and instead] used first names, 'boy', or 'girl', or sometimes even 'n—' . . . Older black people were sometimes

called 'auntie' or 'uncle'. But black people were expected to use Mr, Mrs, or Miss when addressing white people, including adolescents. 'Boss' or 'cap'n' might do for a white man.[11]

Life for Black Americans in Jim Crow United States was precarious at best and terrifying at worst. White legal and cultural apartheid; sanctioned white mob violence, such as the cultural phenomenon of attending 'lynching picnics' or 'watch parties'; white economic structures; structural racism in housing, employment, education, the armed forces, government employment and the like that limited job and economic possibilities: these were but a few of the challenges faced by Black Americans under Jim Crow.

It is of great significance, then, that Hurston's first experiences as a girl growing up in the U.S. South were within an almost exclusively rural, Southern, Black American context. Her experiences as a girl, discovering herself in the context of family and community, matters to how Hurston understood, as well as created, Black folk people and characters. That is, Hurston – like the Black American characters she created – while always already subject to a Jim Crow American system, began her life in a community that was the ostensible inverse of said system: an all-Black community of self-governing, principled, accomplished, capable, aspiring, creative neighbours and relatives. Hurston asserts in her seminal essay 'How It Feels to Be Colored Me' that the hyper-presence and spectre of whiteness and white supremacy did not register in and thus impact on her consciousness fully until she was thirteen years old and away from her home town of Eatonville. Instead, the realization arrived on a steamboat ride to Jacksonville, Florida, and in the context of a largely white worldscape.

Hurston wrote that at thirteen she was sent off to attend boarding school in Jacksonville, and her mode of transportation was a steamboat. What exactly happened to alter Hurston's perception of herself from 'everybody's Zora' to 'a fast brown – warranted not to rub nor run', as she comes to see of herself, goes undetailed in 'How It Feels to Be Colored Me'. Was Hurston accosted by white passengers? Did she, a young teenager away from home for the first time, have to steel herself against the visceral hatred of racist fellow passengers? Was she treated as subhuman, dismissed or outright rejected and ignored? Did someone hit or otherwise mistreat her at a time when she was moving away from all she had ever known, while still mourning the loss of her mother? The particulars of the assault to her spirit are unknown. What is known is that at that time, Hurston's encounters with white Americans, outside of the context and relative safety of her home community, altered her perception of herself – as well as her sense of reality.

Hurston's steamboat ride was a moment of both transformation and loss, where she was confronted by the racialized, gendered and to a degree classist ideologies and actions of the white steamboat occupants. Hurston wrote in 'How It Feels to Be Colored Me' of being rendered not herself but 'colored' during – and, the essay suggests, following – her steamboat ride to Jacksonville.[12] In the essay, Hurston also wrote of herself as 'a born first-nighter' – she was always drawn to wordplay, music and drama.[13] As a girl, she would 'wave at' white Northerners, often voyeuristic in their gaze as they passed through Eatonville.[14] Hurston wrote of how when these white Northerners 'returned my salute, I would say something like this: "Howdy-do-well-I-thank-you-where-you-goin'?"'[15] Hurston adds further that sometimes, after a queer exchange of compliments, she would even 'go a piece of the way' with these white strangers – meaning travel along the road with them – something that would have been highly unusual in the segregated South.[16] One can just imagine the strain on the mind and nerves of her maternal grandmother, Sarah Potts, as she bore witness to Zora's natural ways (Zora was gregarious, curious and friendly as a girl). Hurston wrote in her autobiography that Grandmother Potts blamed John and scolded Lucy for what she regarded as Hurston's personality deficits, including her tendency to fib or to make up stories.

Hurston was born into the era of the so-called New Woman.[17] Through this cultural phenomenon, Hurston's differences were seen via the lens of not just a woman, or a Black woman, but a northern-educated, Southern Black woman. As the anthropologist Esther Newton writes,

The second generation of New Women were born in the 1870s and 1880s and came of age during the opening decades of the twentieth century. This was an extraordinarily distinguished group. Among them we count critics of the family and political radicals Margaret Sanger and Crystal Eastman; women drawn to new artistic fields, such as Berenice Abbott and Isadora Duncan; and lesbian writers such as Gertrude Stein, Willa Cather, Margaret Anderson, Natalie Barney, and Radclyffe Hall.[18]

To that list I would add women such as the renowned dancer and anthropologist Katherine Dunham; the dancer and singer Josephine Baker; the performer Ada 'Bricktop' Smith; the singer Bessie Smith; the poet Gwendolyn Bennett; and, of course, Zora Neale Hurston. It can be extrapolated from Newton (writing exclusively of the white New Women) that the Black New Women, too, sought autonomy and to break with the domestic roles occupied by their mothers.

The early twentieth-century New Woman was educated, young (around her early twenties), independent and capable. She may have sought out an education in favour of marriage or delayed marriage until after her education. She enjoyed her life, whether through partying, dating or pursuing a career. This New Woman could take care of and provide for herself, enjoyed a good time, was a professional and, most of all, was imaged as white. The 'New Negro' – which coalesced with the New Woman in the person, ideas and creativity of Zora Neale Hurston – represented a modern Black subjectivity. According to Jeffrey C. Stewart's *The New Negro: The Life of Alain Locke* (2018), it was a term resonant in Black American culture during the early twentieth century. However, the term 'New Negro' gained articulation and codification in the writing of Hurston's future mentor and professor at Howard University, the African American philosopher Alain Locke, in his edited anthology of poetry, stories and essays *The New Negro: Voices of the Harlem Renaissance* (1925), a work in which Hurston is included.

Born free like her mother – a literate Black woman educator – and to a charismatic and gifted orator of a father, Hurston was expected to excel in all aspects of her life, though perhaps especially

Hurston, *c.* 1919–22, poised and ready for the opportunities to come from her studies at Howard University.

Hurston, *c.* 1919–23, while a student at Howard University.

academically. With transfer credits from Howard, Hurston matriculated at Barnard College in 1925, graduating in 1928 with a degree in anthropology, which she studied under Franz Boas, the founder of the discipline and a professor at neighbouring Columbia University, of which Barnard is part. In her first or second semester at Barnard, Hurston wrote a paper that was shared with Boas, whose interest was so piqued that he invited Hurston to meet him. In her first four years as a transplant to New York, not only did 'mama's child', as Hurston writes of herself in her autobiography, garner intellectual and creative support from such distinguished African American scholars and educators as Locke and Charles S. Johnson, as well as Boas, but she managed to graduate with an elite education and did so virtually free of debt.[19] 'Hurston was an exception,' writes Patricia Hill Collins, 'for prior to 1950, few African-American women earned advanced degrees.'[20]

In January 1925, Hurston had arrived in New York from Washington, DC, homeless and without means. She was 35 years old, but passing herself off as 25. Hurston's performance of youth, which she did perhaps as early as 1905, was generally accepted. The common consensus was that Hurston seemed advanced for her age – and she was. When she enrolled at Barnard, Hurston was required to take language classes. She chose French, perhaps with foreknowledge of her budding creative and research interests in the Global South, including in countries such as Haiti, Jamaica and the Bahamas. By the following summer, Hurston was in the field, collecting on a fellowship to the tune of $1,400, underwritten by Carter G. Woodson, founder of the Association for the Study of African American Life and History (ASALH), an academic association still in operation today. Thus Hurston quickly transitioned from a virtually unknown part-time university student to an award-winning Black woman intellectual. She was also waking up to and walking in a world of intellectual giants. Already, her mentors included leading men in their fields, such as Locke, Johnson, Boas and Woodson. Hurston by this time had likewise garnered friendships with Black writers and intellectuals who, like her, would form the vanguard of the 'new' Black art – the Harlem Renaissance. These included the poets Langston Hughes, Countee Cullen and Helene Johnson, and novelists Dorothy West and Jessie Fauset. Hurston also sought and received occasional counsel from the leading African American sociologist of the period, W.E.B. Du Bois. She was a woman in a rarefied community, and she created for herself not simply a seat at the table but, more importantly, a central and centring location from which to see and to imagine, and from which she too could be seen and known.

Hurston represented the best and the brightest of her race and nation, and was a fitting example of the New Negro conceptualized by Locke in his *The New Negro*. She also represented aspects of the 'Talented Tenth', the upper echelon of educated Black society that

Hurston in 1938 at 47 years old, passing as 37. The photograph was taken as part of a series by Hurston's friend and occasional benefactor Carl Van Vechten.

would point the way for the lower, labouring classes, which Du Bois, the first African American to graduate with a PhD from Harvard, theorized in his generative essay of the same name, a foundational document of Black intellectual studies that was included in *The Negro Problem: A Series of Articles by Representative American Negroes of Today* (1903). However, neither Locke's nor Du Bois's concepts of twentieth-century Black subjectivity could fully encapsulate Hurston. This is in part because the person at the centre of both intellectuals' concepts was a Black man, not a Black woman.

2
Opportunity

In 1917–18, just shy of ten years before she graduated from Barnard College, Hurston was enrolled in night school as a high school student. During a class at Morgan Academy, then a high school for Black Americans in Baltimore, Maryland, she sat listening to her English teacher, Dwight O. W. Holmes, recite – or, more correctly, embody – the poem 'Kubla Khan' (1797) by the British Romantic writer and poet Samuel Taylor Coleridge. Hurston wrote in *Dust Tracks on a Road* that she came alive during the reading. Holmes, an African American, had, by his reading of Coleridge's most famous poem, invited Hurston into a world that she would in that instant claim as her own. It was a world of the written *and* the spoken word; for Hurston, who soon after became part of the world of writing and literature, it was an entry point into the drama, beauty and possibility of language. This positive, affirming moment of educational learning and engagement was one that awakened the consciousness of the student who would become the writer and intellectual Zora Neale Hurston.

Four years later, in 1921, Hurston had transferred to and enrolled at the prestigious and historically Black Howard University in Washington, DC. Hurston continued to present herself as ten years younger than her actual age. Her rationale for doing so seems likely to have been acculturation, and perhaps also because Hurston was the product of a national culture that favoured youth. She was so good at disguising the fact that she was a decade older than her classmates and friends that as late as the 1990s, in an interview conducted for the documentary *Zora Neale Hurston: Jump at the*

A young Zora with friends, probably classmates at Morgan Academy in Baltimore, Maryland, *c.* 1917–23.

Sun (2008), the novelist and one-time friend of Hurston's Dorothy West commented that she was still uncertain as to Hurston's actual age. West suspected Hurston was at least ten years older than she asserted.

Between working as a waitress at the gender-exclusive, all-white Cosmos Club in Washington, DC, where she waited on leading white male scientists and philosophers, and working as a manicurist at a Black-owned, whites-only barbershop near the Howard campus, Hurston attended first high school and then undergraduate studies at Howard, part-time, until her relocation to New York in 1925. As well as working, attending classes at Howard (where she was an English major), pledging the sorority Zeta Phi Beta and courting the man who would become her first husband, Hurston also wrote, and had joined Howard University's exclusive, student-run literary magazine *Stylus*, even participating as co-editor (under the guidance of Alain Locke, who was a faculty advisor for the journal). According to Yuval Taylor in his book *Zora and Langston: A Story of Friendship and Betrayal* (2019), Locke considered Hurston to be among his 'best and brightest students', a sentiment he conveyed to his friend and fellow scholar Charles S. Johnson, to whom he had recommended some of Hurston's earliest writing.[1]

Hurston's first published work was in a 1921 issue of *Stylus*, edited by Locke. Locke was arguably the leading African American philosopher of the time and was responsible for not only fostering the phrase 'New Negro' but mediating relationships between young Black talents (those who would become Harlem Renaissance literati) and the wealthy white benefactor Charlotte Osgood Mason, who would later become Hurston's employer and patron. Locke read Hurston's work and saw talent as well as possibility. She would be part of the vanguard of the New Negro that he was imagining, and the new Black art these individuals would create.

Hurston published two pieces in the 1921 issue of *Stylus*: a three-stanza poem entitled 'Home' and the short story 'John Redding Goes to Sea'. Both works show how Hurston the writer was compelled by the intimate and interested in the individual self in relation to others. The end rhyme of 'Home' reveals the influence of the British Romantics on Hurston, who throughout her career published little poetry:

> And brush away the somber shrouds,
> And show the lining of the clouds![2]

The emotionalism of the poem as well as Hurston's invocation of the sublime in deference to nature show the impact of Romanticism on her writing – though the impact is complicated by Hurston's autodidactic grounding in Greek and Norse mythology and in

Howard University, probably late 19th century, stereograph image.

African American folktales. She expresses, significantly, the nineteenth-century Romantic idea of the self in relation to the natural world and in flight from the world of man(kind). It is also possible for readers to see the influence of American Romanticism on Hurston's early writing, with its emphasis on the individual self and its centring of quest narratives (think, for example, of the *Adventures of Huckleberry Finn*, or the tonality, surprise and longing in the poetry of Emily Dickinson). 'Home' suggests a Black woman speaker ostensibly longing to return to a home that is no longer there; it exists now only as a memory – and, in the writer's hands, as poetry. It reads as both a lament and a song, or lyric, to a thing cherished and lost. Home is a physical space of nurturance, comfort and light, a physical dwelling, but also something ephemeral – for Hurston, 'home' is family.

By the third stanza of the poem, the ever-present and repeating 'I' has come into focus. This 'I' is shrouded in sombreness; the speaker's experience of life is one that produces the wish to 'flee!' Without the existence or even the possibility of a home 'where pleasing fancy loves to roam', a home 'full of light', the speaker's experience is one in which mankind's cruelty is clear; where one's faith is constantly shaken.[3] The poem thus reads as a tragedy and as a lament. It is a poem of opposite extremes of experience and of opposite extremes of emotion. Notably absent is the amalgamation of Standard English and Black vernacular English (for example, African American Vernacular English) for which Hurston is known in her fiction and, to a degree, non-fiction. As a newly published writer and a fresh voice in fiction, she was keeping to the high formalism of the American and British Romantics, in terms of both tonality and style.

In a reprint of the poem included in *Speak, So You Can Speak Again* (2004), compiled by the Estate of Zora Neale Hurston and edited by Hurston's niece, Lucy Anne Hurston, a note is included that readers are to assume is written in Hurston's own hand: 'Just a bubbling over of a melancholy heart – momentarily.'[4] As Hurston says of herself in 'How It Feels to Be Colored Me', she does not 'belong to the sobbing school of Negrohood who hold that nature somehow has given them a lowdown dirty deal and whose feelings are all hurt about it'.[5] Hurston might have continued: neither does she seem to belong to *any* sobbing school, regardless of gender, sex, sexuality, race, ethnicity, nationality or socio-economic class or caste. This to say that Hurston understood most readily that she must be uniquely *human*, and not confined to much stricter labels than that, and live a life of and appreciation for the gifts granted to her.

In her early poetry, as in all her writing, Hurston stated her difference not only as a Black woman artist but, significantly, an intellectual who was finely attuned to the currents and undercurrents of u.s. society and culture. As early as 1921, Hurston's ideas about self and art are in evidence: for her, there must be vibrancy; the ecstasy of play, physical, verbal and otherwise; and a sense of one's life and art as cosmic.

As an English student during her five years of part-time study at Howard University, Hurston was learning aspects of formal literary criticism alongside writing and submitting her creative work to *Stylus*. She was most likely receiving feedback on her creative work from Locke, as she would continue to do after graduating. Hurston's brief 'bubbling over' of 'melancholy', as she writes of her poem, suggests that the feeling of melancholia becomes the vehicle through which the writer is both compelled to create and through which she expresses emotion. If Hurston cannot freely express herself in her daily living, if she cannot fully feel her feelings without the real possibility of abandonment or insult, what she *can* do is channel through art those repressed emotions and unexpressed experiences that 'mar my days,/ And dim for me the sun's loved rays'.

The shared tone of 'John Redding Goes to Sea' and 'Home' is sombre, and there is yearning at the centre of both works. By 1921, Hurston had been an orphan for a full three years. Both her father's death in a tragic automobile accident in 1918 in Memphis, Tennessee, when his car was hit by an oncoming train, and her mother's death in 1904 had a colossal impact on Hurston, which can be glimpsed in her earliest published pieces. In both the short story and the poem, Hurston expresses desire for something else, something more. The former work suggests a yearning for a life, or life experience, unhampered by oppression, the constriction of cultural and familial expectations and the limitations of convention. In its opening line, Hurston establishes the setting: St Johns River, a northward-flowing river spanning 500 kilometres (310 mi.) of north-central Florida. Because John Redding, the story's imaginative and dreamy protagonist, grew up with the river just a 'scarce three hundred feet [90 m] from his back door', the river and its edge (the horizon) inspire his dreams.[6]

'John Redding Goes to Sea' tells of a 'little brown boy', John, who 'loved to wander down to the water's edge, and [cast] in dry twigs, [and] watch them sail away downstream to Jacksonville, the sea, the wild world'.[7] As Hurston writes, 'John Redding wanted to follow them.'[8] John grew up around commerce, itinerant pier workers and travellers from Jacksonville and beyond, all of whom suggested intrigue and excitement for a boy prone to wandering – John's mother is convinced her son is hexed by some conjurer who has cursed her son to wander all his days. The short story reads to an extent as an allegory for young Zora's life.

When he is a married young man, John decides he can no longer remain in his home town and must seek out his destiny in the great beyond. He must leave behind his young wife, though he intends to provide for her and return to see her when possible. For John, there is no way around the marital abandonment. John's mother threatens to disown him, and his wife threatens to leave him and return to her family. However, John's father, a man of similar character and temperament to his son and with whom John shares a deep bond – which includes intimate one-on-one conversations about life, marriage and women – is sympathetic towards his son and therefore engages, on his son's behalf, in a family battle with his wife and daughter-in-law. As a result, John postpones an offer to join the u.s. Navy by one year to appease his mother and wife. While volunteering (or being volunteered?) to help restore a bridge during a hurricane, John dies in a freak accident. Thus, John lives the entirety of his short life longing to flee the very town in which he will prematurely die, being prevented from doing so by his (albeit conditional) responsibility and devotion to his mother and his wife. Tradition, a sense of familial responsibility, guilt and the misunderstanding, limitations and fears of others keep John from pursuing his lifelong dream. Though John's mother requests that his body be recovered from the river in which he drowned, his father demands that his son be set adrift and buried at sea. In this way, the father ensures that, albeit in death, his son's one wish and desire is fulfilled: that of escape to a bigger, more expansive world.

John's story is a tragedy, but perhaps Hurston would not have considered it as such. More likely, she might have seen John's story as tragicomic or realist in nature. Like the twigs John cast about in St Johns River as a boy, and later as a man, John got 'caught in the weeds' of life; his being and the wants of his wife and his mother collided, much like John's body collided with the 'logs [that] struck' and killed him.[9] He is waylaid owing to a decision of the mind, albeit with the emotional prompting of the women in his family, and not long after succumbs to a violent death.

In 'John Redding Goes to Sea', the main character is an explorer by nature and is truncated emotionally and physically, ultimately surrendering to a life constrained by the desires of his wife and mother, as well as by his commitments as a husband, son and community member. Even his ideas of the horizon are limited. Hurston enlists a third-person omniscient narrator to tell John's story of limitations. As a child, John sometimes dreamed 'he was a prince, riding away in a gorgeous carriage'. The narrator continues, 'Often he was a knight bestride a fiery charger prancing down the white shell road that led to distant lands. At other times he was a steamboat captain piloting his craft down the St. Johns River to where the sky seemed to touch the water.' The narrator adds, 'No matter what he dreamed or who he fancied himself to be, he always ended riding away to the horizon; for in his childish ignorance he thought this to be farthest land.'[10] That is, even as a young boy John dreams of adventure, distant shores and escape. Still, however, his dreams show the limitations of his imagination and his lived reality. The story suggests the limitations and constrictions that the status quo can impose on Black families. Moreover, it shows how Black sexual politics and people's actions that emanate from guilt, and a sense of duty rather than desire, can jettison any hope of forging a new path. Only the father understands John's desire to go to sea, and, ultimately, he sets his son free. The story suggests that John's desires as a boy and man engender painful remembrances in John's father of his own boyhood and manhood. To ward off the pain, John's father hides aspects of his past from his son, thus figuratively rendering the son isolated with his desires. The story suggests that in the father's attempts to shield John from his own disappointment, as a Black man and as a husband, the father renders John vulnerable to the demands of the women in the family – that is, John's wife and mother – and to the demands of custom. In what is their last conversation, John and his father open up to one another. John says to his father,

> You know, papa, sometimes I reckon my longing to get away makes me feel this way . . . I feel that I am just earth's soil, lying helpless to move myself but thinking. I seem to hear herds of big beasts like horses and cows thundering over me, and rains beating down; and winds sweeping furiously over – all acting upon me, but me, well, just soil, feeling but not able to take part in it all.[11]

John, clearly suffering existential malaise and, it would seem, depression, continues:

> Then a soft wind like love passes over and warms me, and a summer rain comes down like understanding and softens me, and I push a blade of grass or a flower or maybe a pine. That's the ground thinking. Plants are ground thoughts. Because the soil can't move itself. Whenever I see little whirls of dust sailing down the road I always step aside. I don't want to stop them cause they are on their shining way, moving. Oh, yes. I'm a dreamer. I have such wonderfully complete dreams . . . they never come true, but even as my dreams fade I have others.[12]

In addition to being a dreamer, John shows that he is a poet. This conversation between John and his father occurs shortly before John's early demise, having taken his father's place on a volunteer job. What is important here is that both men are able to share with one another, not only as son and father but as human beings, their desire to seek a richer and far greater experience of life. John's father makes his son aware that they share the same feelings and that they are aligned in life – and, by the story's end, in death as well. Significantly, Hurston's first short story centres on a relationship between a Black son and father who lose one another to poverty, a sense of duty and tradition, and early death. In many ways, the story doubles as Zora and her mother's own, with the exception of their gender and the associated norms. It might also double as Zora and her father, who Hurston lost just three years prior to the publication of 'John Redding Goes to Sea'.

Hurston's *Stylus* writings showcase a writer on the cusp of breaking out of a life that became, after the death of her mother and the abandonment by her father, more and more confined and desolate. The Hurston who was writing and publishing in 1921 had made a way for herself where there had previously seemed no path to take. And, notably, she managed to fashion a life and engender a writing career for herself that wound up having a far-reaching impact on Black women readers and writers the world over. Hurston's short story 'John Redding Goes to Sea' and her poem 'Home' both reflect a desire in the speaker-protagonist to flee. Whereas in Hurston's poem the desire is to 'flee' towards a calm, welcoming and light-filled home, in her short story the main character seeks to flee home itself and all the limitations that accrue there. For John Redding, home means family responsibility and obligations doled out by wives and mothers. Yet while John's home – considered both as dwelling place and as family – remains after his death, the speaker in Hurston's poem can only remember what has passed; the warmth of home is no longer available to them. While different in terms of genre and characters, there is profound loss at the centre of both works, and that loss is connected in every way to family.

A psychoanalytic reading of 'John Redding Goes to Sea' might suggest that for the 28-year-old Hurston writing in 1921, home might have been missing quite a bit. Her mother had died more than fifteen years earlier; her family was dispersed; and her family home as it was, with her mother, had been a thing of the past since 1905. Even before her father's death in 1918, Hurston had long since been abandoned by him. She must have felt the loss of her father powerfully, but she did not attend his funeral. Home, peace, love, sunlight and the desire to flee were, it seems, at the forefront of the writer's mind at the time of the writing and publication of short story and poem.

Hurston wrote 'Home' in a high formal English that is reminiscent of earlier eras and styles, rather than the free verse of, say, Walt Whitman or the improvisation and syncopation of her contemporary Langston Hughes. In 'John Redding Goes to Sea', however, Hurston displayed a stylistic choice that she stayed with throughout her writing career: incorporating both Standard and Black English in her fiction writing.

Hurston left Eatonville at the age of fourteen – a newly motherless girl abandoned by her father who had hired herself out to white Southerners as domestic help – and in 1927, at the age of 37, she returned there a changed person, on the brink of a professional and creative career that would span three decades and end only upon her death in 1960. In *Zora Neale Hurston: A Literary Biography*, Robert Hemenway further provides that Hurston's return to Eatonville in 1927 was 'under the aegis of an internationally known anthropologist', and she was 'affiliated with a prestigious institution of higher learning, and supported by America's leading black historian, Carter G. Woodson, founder and director of the Association for the Study of Negro Life and History'. Back in Florida, she would approach 'as a social scientist what she had lived as a child'.[13]

Before we look at how this period in Eatonville influenced Hurston, let us focus on 1925, when she had just relocated from Washington, DC, to Harlem, New York, where she would quickly make a life for herself as a budding writer while a student at Barnard. On the night of Friday, 1 May 1925, there was a great gathering of Black and white literary, cultural, philanthropic and publishing figures in New York City – a gathering that also included a cadre of up-and-coming African American writers. Among them were Hurston, Langston Hughes and Countee Cullen. It was a momentous occasion for several reasons. This integrated, elite and powerful community of individuals who had invested in and were partially financing the event marked a zenith of what has variously been referred to as the New Negro Arts Movement, the Harlem Renaissance and a New Renaissance in Black Art, a period spanning the late 1900s to the late 1920s. The period was characterized by a heightened interest in and production of African American art, literature, theatre and culture by Black elites and up-and-coming Black artists, and by members of the largely white publishing industry.

At the time, Hurston was an orphan with a high school diploma and four years of part-time attendance at Howard University, which was then the Black intellectual centre of the academic world. It was a place that afforded Hurston not only a prestigious higher education but knowledge of and access to outlets for her writing. While at Howard, Hurston joined the historically Black women's sorority Zeta Phi Beta, published her first writings and, through Alain Locke, was brought to the attention of the leading African American sociologist Charles S. Johnson and his academic journal *Opportunity: A Journal of Negro Life*. Johnson was director of the National Urban League, a civil rights organization founded in 1910 in New York City and for which *Opportunity* was the literary and cultural arm. The event that night in May 1925 was the second annual literary awards ceremony sponsored by the journal. Hurston had been encouraged to submit her work to *Opportunity*'s literary competition by Locke, who was the emcee for the awards ceremony that evening and who had worked closely with Johnson for a time. Hurston did not secure first place in any of the literary awards, but she did secure the attention of most of those in attendance.

Johnson, later the first African American president of Fisk University in Nashville, Tennessee, became a central figure in

Hurston looking poised, slim and youthful in clothes suggestive of early 20th-century flappers.

Hurston's life. He was by all accounts a learned and pragmatic man who believed in the possibility and downright necessity of interracial Black and white American coalition work in the service of the advancement of the full civil and human rights of African Americans – advancement within, that is, a largely resistant and aggressive white supremacist legal, political, social and cultural regime. *Opportunity* was pre-eminent among Black publications at the time, including the NAACP's *Crisis*. What made *Opportunity* stand out was that Johnson sought submissions, whether essays, poetry, short stories or other media, that demonstrated the diversity and complexity of Black Americans, without insisting that Black writers cast their Black figures in an always positive light. That is, Johnson welcomed Black art that was representative of Black life, without regard for the white gaze. In his role as editor, which he held from 1923 to 1928, he published the early works of Hurston, Hughes, Claude McKay, Dorothy West and Helene Johnson, to name but a few of the writers who would become luminaries of Black arts, life and literature both during and following the Harlem Renaissance. In effect, at *Opportunity*, and even in his position as director of the National Urban League, of which the magazine was an extension, Johnson helped to usher in the new wave of Black American writers who would come to be known as New Negro artists.

Johnson was well connected to both Black and white American elites in New York, many if not all of whom attended his magazine's awards dinner on 1 May 1925. The 316 guests included the Jewish novelist Fannie Hurst; the journalist, novelist and amateur photographer Carl Van Vechten;[14] and the anti-suffragist Annie Nathan Meyer, who was also a founder of Barnard College. Also in attendance were leading white writers and intellectuals and, significantly, white publishers. The African American novelist and intellectual James Weldon Johnson – who in 1900, together with his brother the composer J. Rosamond Johnson, wrote 'Lift Ev'ry Voice and Sing', commonly known as the Black national anthem – was in attendance, as was the African American singer Paul Robeson and the young sociologist E. Franklin Frazier. These famous and well-to-do guests, some of whom doubled as judges for the literary awards, mingled with the nominees and award-winners and other fresh Black creative talents, as was Johnson's arrangement and desire. What happened in the process of this interracial, interclass and intercultural mingling was the establishment of professional and personal relationships, such as the one between Hurston and Meyer, two American women from vastly different racial, ethnic, social, cultural, class and caste backgrounds – not to mention regions – but who shared some similarities in terms of desired profession (that of writer) and family circumstances, both having experienced the dissolution of their biological family following the deaths of their mothers when they were girls.

Despite Hurston not placing first in any category (she instead came in second place), she still won the most awards that night. Her first play *Color Struck*, a short dramatic work, was one of the winning titles. In it, readers are introduced to a brown-skinned Black woman by the name of Emmaline. Emmaline's main affliction is that she is 'color struck' – that is, she has imbibed the racism extant in her nation and become convinced of an innate inferiority or superiority according to skin tones within Black communities. In Emmaline's culture, lighter-skinned Black Americans hold more value than darker-skinned Black Americans because of their approximation to American whiteness. Emmaline has accepted this ugly reality as an incontrovertible truth. The play's central Black woman character is convinced her beau is interested in the lighter-skinned Black women among their group. Since she values lighter-skinned Black women and devalues darker-skinned Black women, she expects the same of her beau. Thus, in the play, Emmaline acts the fool and not only loses face but loses her beloved man in the process of hating another woman for something as unoriginal as, the play suggests, her skin tone.

Here, as in other places throughout her body of work, Hurston puts a spotlight on colourism and intra-racism within African American communities. Despite Hurston winning accolades for the work, Warren J. Carson writes that *Color Struck*, consists of 'four sketches strung together in a rather loose fashion' and argues that the work 'does not show Hurston at her best'.[15] Carson says that 'the scenes are not sufficiently developed and the characters, for the most part, are not convincingly delineated . . . from a technical standpoint, the play is probably too brief to justify the difficulty that would be incurred in staging it.'[16] He thus argues that *Color Struck* is 'the work of a young and immature writer'.[17] Carson celebrates that the play showcases how 'Hurston recognize[d] dialect's worth and employs it to its fullest in presenting reality as she saw it.'[18] He adds, 'Her ability with regard to language is certainly a mark of her genius.'[19] Hurston's emphasis on courtship and kinship rituals among the labouring Black classes shows up time and again in her work. Likewise, the centring of Black dance and language traditions that occurs in all her work is seen first in *Color Struck* in her presentation of the dance celebration known as the cakewalk.

The cakewalk, as a dance competition and celebration, Hurston suggests, belongs to the Black folk tradition (which she would capture and chronicle in her first folklore collection, *Mules and Men* (1935)). *Color Struck* showcases Black individuals in their finery, enjoying a dance and each other. The play foregrounds a Black Southern community, as well as the existence of Jim Crow laws: *Color Struck* opens with a scene in a segregated train car. The play's main character, Emmaline, is a 'bitter' Black woman obsessed with and repelled by mixed-race women in particular, whom she refers to angrily as 'them half whites'.[20] Emmaline cries, 'They gets everything everybody else wants! The men, the jobs – everything! The whole world is got a sign on it. Wanted: Light colored. Us blacks was made for cobble stones.'[21] There is the suggestion of a recognition of colour caste, which is to say the socio-economic status and cultural valuation accorded to Black Americans by Black and other Americans as a result of their light skin and European or Anglo features. At the heart of *Color Struck* there is an examination of this favouring of the mixed-race (Black and white) subject over the African-descended Black American (that is, without known or noticeable European bloodlines).

As a character, Emmaline is a feminized mouthpiece who articulates the lack of parity for Black people – and Black women specifically – within romantic relationships, as well as economics. Who says Hurston was not political in her creative writing? One does not have to be overt in their beliefs to be political, and art that is subtle in its politics and leanings is art at its absolute best. But more than conveying the unequal status of Black women, Emmaline's character also draws attention to the intra-racism and colour bias that disfavoured mixed-race women within the context of an all-Black community, and the influence of a jealousy and fear – rooted in hatred – that finds its source in a felt sense of the unfairness and constriction of living under a white heteropatriarchal, sexist, misogynist, classist, racist and ableist postbellum u.s. society and culture. Emmaline is a mirror for

Hurston's contemporaneous readers, and a window for her future readers.

Indeed, it is Emmaline who is 'colour struck' and untrusting of anyone who loves her, but tellingly – or perhaps especially – this distrust is apparent when she is in the presence of mixed-race girls and women, including her own daughter. Emmaline is blind to her own condition, and this unfortunate circumstance leads not only to the death of her one child, the mixed-race daughter born out of wedlock, but to the loss of the love of her life, 'a light brown-skinned man', as Hurston writes of him in the stage notes.

Emmaline does not trust that John (a popular lead character name for Hurston in her writing of the 1920s and '30s) loves her truly, and she instead projects her own biases on to him. When John, early abandoned by but still in love with Emmaline, returns to their home town newly widowed and in search of Emmaline, who he wants to marry, he discovers his beloved has a sickly teenage daughter. It just so happens that the daughter is mixed-race, described by Hurston in the stage notes as 'a mulatto girl'. John professes his love to Emmaline, who is swayed to return to him, but when she notices his concern for her sick daughter, she reads it as sexual lasciviousness and desire. John beseeches Emmaline to seek out the doctor, even giving her his wallet to assist with funding, but she refuses, distrusting of his motives, and ultimately allows her daughter to die. Emmaline is convinced that John, a Black man, cannot contain his sexual impulses and desires in the presence of a mixed-race female. She thus renders John a hypersexualized predator, fixing him in an ostensible white racist gaze – one that is her own. What might Hurston be suggesting here about Black sexual politics, in particular relationships between Black women and those between Black women and Black men? Here, as in other places throughout her body of work, Hurston presages the work of the American Black feminists of the 1970s such as Michele Wallace, Barbara Smith, Audre Lorde and Alice Walker.

Color Struck is a pioneering literary work. Where else in literature (whether American, African American or feminist) do we see such a dynamic? That is, where the focus is on drawing the eye inwards to study Black communities and take stock of the ways in which such communities shored up repressive and stereotyped images of the Black male subject as hypersexual, especially when in close proximity to white femininity (here in the figure of the mixed-race female subject). In *Color Struck*, Hurston presents the tragic figure of a Black woman who is lacking in self-love and wandering blind, incapable of seeing her own worth, unable to see the truth of her value and – in particular – her desirability as a sexual subject for Black men.

In the play, we see early glimpses of the prolific writer and anthropologist who would offer up to the world *Mules and Men*, a first-of-its-kind anthology of u.s. Black folklore, inclusive of spiritual and cultural practices; folk heroes such as John Henry and the biblical figure of Moses; and work songs, courting rituals, children's games and the like. Although Hurston writes in *Mules and Men* that it took time, distance and education for her to be able to see and assess what was always right before her eyes, and within her – that is, her own self-governed Black culture and personhood – her early works suggest that the vision was always present. The suggestion of the play is that it is the women as much as the men who are colour struck. Like the treatment of the biracial character Squeak in Alice Walker's novel *The Color Purple* (1982), many of the Black women in the community are cold towards and apparently jealous of Effie, the 'mulatto' character in the play.

On that May night in New York City, at the *Opportunity* awards dinner, Hurston took second place in the category of short fiction for her short story 'Spunk'. 'Spunk' is the story of Spunk Banks, a man who cuckolds and then murders Joe, the owner of the village store. 'Joe knew his wife had passed that way. He knew that the men lounging in the general store had seen her, moreover, he knew that the men knew *he* knew,' Hurston writes.[22] Joe is chagrined. Ultimately however it is Joe who loses his life as he is overpowered by Spunk Banks. The story brings together comedy, hoodoo, the unexplained, dialect, gossip as a source of information and ideas about womanhood, manhood and marriage or courting. It suggests that Joe's ghost takes his revenge first on Spunk and then on his cheating wife, Lena, both of whom die by the story's end. Walter, one of the village voices – all of whom are Black men – says of Spunk, 'I'm skeered of dat man when he gits hot. He'd beat you full of button holes as quick as he's look atcher.'[23] The moral question is: does it take spunk to use your looks to cuckold and your pistol to kill a man because you want to marry his wife, as Spunk Banks does? Or is having spunk the action of going after the man who cuckolded and embarrassed you in front of your community despite knowing you are under-armed and bound to be beaten badly by your rival, as Joe does? Most compelling is the community's belief that Joe's ghost returns to exact his revenge. This implies a belief system within the community that accommodates secular and non-secular aspects of the supernatural.

At the *Opportunity* awards dinner, Hurston met the woman who would help her achieve her dream of furthering her higher education: Annie Nathan Meyer. When Hurston struggled to secure enough funding to support her attendance at Barnard College, Meyer and her friends outsourced work to her, employing Hurston for domestic duties. Meyer also helped to obtain Hurston employment with the then hugely popular writer Fannie Hurst, first as a secretary and then as a driver. In late 1926, Meyer would step in personally to provide Hurston with a scholarship, so that by spring 1927 Hurston was enrolled full-time at Barnard College.

Hurston's letters demonstrate that Hurston's first semester at Barnard – a privileged, elite, all-white and single-sex Northern educational environment – was challenging for several reasons. She struggled with funding, and wrestled with obtaining the required clothing and other college necessities. Her grades fluctuated depending on the subject. It seemed less a matter of difficulty than of interest (similar to her time at Howard University, where a gym class garnered an F while literature classes garnered As and Bs). Hurston also studied French at Barnard and took tennis and golf lessons for sports and exercise classes. As the university's first African American student, Hurston experienced not only resistance and class and caste isolation but racial isolation, insults and bigotry.

According to her letters from this period, Hurston's classmates in her French courses would laugh when she recited her vocabulary. One wonders what was so funny to Hurston's white women classmates, unaccustomed to sharing equal space with a Black woman. Was it Hurston's pronunciation, owing to her Southern roots? Was it the fact that a Black woman was speaking French? Was it that a Black woman was attempting something that they too were trying, and possibly failing, to do? Was it class and caste bias informed by white American racism and white American cultural imperialism? Was it their own cultural and racial (and linguistic) elitism? Or was it simply funny? Hurston writes in a letter of 17 December 1925 to Annie Nathan Meyer that 'one of those laughers has asked to quiz with me.'[24] She continues in the letter to the college's co-founder, 'I knew getting mad would not help any. I had to get my lessons so well that their laughter would seem silly.' In addition to being ridiculed by her white women classmates, Hurston was talked out of attending *the* social event of Barnard College – the annual junior prom, which was held at the Ritz-Carlton – by Meyer. This was owing to Hurston's racial difference from her white classmates. Instead of showing offence, however, Hurston, who was it seems excited about the possibility of attending the prom, feigned indifference, writing further in her 17 December letter to Meyer, 'I am not that ritzy yet.' She followed up by stating, 'Of course I don't want to make any false steps . . . [and] am most fortunate in having you to help me before I sprout donkey ears.'[25]

By the second year of her enrolment at Barnard, Hurston was a student of Franz Boas, the founder of the modern discipline of anthropology and chair of that department at neighbouring Columbia University. Hurston was surely Boas's first African American woman student, if not his first African American student. The two would work together, on and off, into the 1930s, during and following Hurston's time at Barnard. Boas was a 'mentor and advisor' for Hurston just as he was a mentor for another leading figure in Black intellectual, literary and cultural studies: W.E.B. Du Bois, a thinker whose influence on Hurston can be seen in both her acceptance and – more often than not – rejection of his ideas on

Black peoples and Black cultures. Hurston attended Barnard as a transfer student from Howard University, where she had majored in English. At Barnard, however, Hurston changed majors to the new discipline of anthropology, studying under Boas. According to Vernon J. Williams, as a researcher and scholar, Boas had a 'revulsion against racism' and advocated 'cultural relativism'.[26] A cultural relativist perspective would be incongruent with racist notions of a people or culture as diminished, substandard or just plain wrong. This suggests then that Boas approached his discipline, and subjects, as attuned to the difference and aware (if not free of) his own standpoint and possible bias.

The scholar Valerie Smith proffers that Boas was 'one of the earliest anthropologists to study black folklore in the United States' and 'believed that racial identity was located in indigenous cultural practices'. Boas saw that 'knowledge of such practices had the power to counteract prevalent notions that African heritage was a source of shame.'[27] bell hooks writes in *Yearning* (1990) that anthropological study, 'once defined as the "study of alien beings", captured the imagination of Zora Neale Hurston when she was seeking a course of academic study that would be compatible with her longing to write'. However, as hooks notes, 'Hurston found the classroom structure a confining place.' By contrast, she 'found the academic environment [to be] one that stretched and expanded her intellectual horizons'.[28] hooks adds: 'Coming to anthropology, [Hurston] was to discover an academic course of study wherein she could express her passion for black culture, where it could be acknowledged, legitimated scholarship worthy of further exploration.'[29]

Hurston's choice of mentor and Boas's choice of mentee seemed predestined, but it was fostered by Hurston, as were all of Hurston's working relationships. As hooks writes, 'The Barnard experience had given Hurston an academic framework that allowed her to critically assess the past; after taking that assessment it was necessary for [Hurston] to bridge the distance.'[30] Hurston collected folk songs, children's games, courting rituals and religious practices from across the southeastern portion of the United States, in particular Florida, Alabama and Louisiana, specifically in New

Orleans, where she underwent a voodoo conversion. Hurston's participation in the voodoo ritual signalled a major departure from her academic training – especially as a Boas-trained anthropologist disciplined towards objectivity in her research and approach. As Yuval Taylor writes, 'Everything changed once [Hurston] arrived in New Orleans in August 1928 and made contact with the voodoo practitioners.'[31] Hurston 'knew well that she was departing in a radical way not only from her previous folklore collecting, but also from the practice of any previous researcher'.[32] Taylor adds, 'nothing could have been further from Zora's life in Harlem than this, and it is impossible to imagine anyone else she knew . . . taking part in such a ritual.'[33] It was evident that 'this [conversion] was not just a challenge, an adventure, a lark,' but 'a deadly serious religious rite requiring Zora's total immersion in practices of extraordinary strangeness'.[34] After her conversion, Hurston spent five months in New Orleans as an understudy to the religion. Robert Hemenway, Hurston's first biographer, writes that the five months between August and December 1928 served to transform Hurston 'from an enthusiastic artist-folklorist into a mature, thoughtful scholar'.[35]

Imagine the appeal of Hurston for Boas. Hurston was still pretending to be ten years younger than her 35 years; she was eager, smart, charismatic, a new transplant from the South; and she clearly had perspective. Hurston had studied literature and drama as an undergraduate at Howard. Here, at Barnard and with Boas, was her opportunity to both research and help shape a bourgeoning discipline as a student and as a practitioner. By the summer of 1927, Boas was sufficiently satisfied with Hurston as a student that he, along with Carter G. Woodson, helped to sponsor Hurston's first expedition in the field, in her hometown of Eatonville, Florida.

Mary Helen Washington writes that Eatonville was 'a gold mine for a folklorist, a rich storehouse of authentic tales, songs, and folkways of black people – unresearched by any black scholar until Hurston'.[36] Heading back to the town was a chance, as Washington continues, to begin a 'unique effort . . . to tell the tales, sing the songs, do the dances, and repeat the raucous saying and doings of the Negro farthest down'.[37] For Hurston, this experience was monumental, since 'it was from this material that she would fashion her career as a folklorist and novelist.'[38]

Hurston was excited about the opportunity to put into practice much of the intellectual and scientific work she undertook while a student of Boas – and surely to go beyond and contribute to the research and scholarship she had accessed via his instruction. Hurston must also have been eager to make use of her talents at writing, for which she had won prizes and relative 'fame' just a few years prior. As Hemenway writes, 'in a sense, [Hurston's] career as a folklorist ended when she finished with her field notes, and after the fall of 1932 she usually conceived of herself as a creative writer – even when writing about folklore.'[39] Hurston's work collecting folklore, all of which was owned and tightly held on to by Charlotte Osgood Mason, her benefactor at the time, would later be culled primarily for her fiction, although occasionally for her non-fiction writing, and formed the basis for much of *Mules and Men*.

Hurston sought out and won the favour, as well as the financial backing, of several white benefactors. While this is also true of other Black writers and artists during the Harlem Renaissance and after, such as Alain Locke and Langston Hughes, Hurston has been criticized both during her lifetime and long after for fostering interracial, interclass and intercultural financial relationships of economic opportunity and dependence. Patriarchy. Misogyny. Sexism. Anti-Blackness. Colourism. Elitism. Classism. Intra-racism. As a Black woman writer determined to make a life for herself through the production of art, Hurston would never escape criticism – as she writes in 'How It Feels to Be Colored Me', she knows that 'for any act of mine, I shall get twice as much praise or twice as much blame.'[40] Hurston is aware, as are her contemporary readers, that there is more to any praise or criticism of her than meets the eye. This was her reality as a practising writer and folklorist who happened to be Black and Southern-born, and who lived during a time when everything she was and represented – by virtue of her race and ethnicity, class and caste, regional roots, gender and sex, and material existence as a writer – was considered on a larger national and cultural scale to be abhorrent.

What options did she have? She fostered relationships with people who were drawn to her intelligence, exuberance, natural talent, charisma and light. Hurston was an imaginative, rambunctious and smart girl born into the poor or peasant class. She grew into an intelligent, determined and practical Black woman, a scholarship student who during her time at Barnard was the university's first and only Black student (shortly after her graduation in 1928, Barnard implemented a quota of two African American students). She negotiated and navigated existences between primarily Northern-situated Black and white intellectual and cultural elites, and Southern-situated rural and labouring-class Blacks. To say she was adaptable is to put it mildly. It might also help explain her ability to maintain relationships, for some time, with wealthy white members of the elite such as Meyer and Mason. After the famed awards dinner of May 1925, Hurston's life would never be the same.

3

Curiosity

In the span of three years, between 1925 and 1928, Hurston went from being a jobless and homeless – albeit with prospects – new transplant from the u.s. South to the North, to an Ivy-educated, celebrated writer, folklorist and anthropologist. This was no easy or uncomplicated feat for Hurston; rather, it was a gargantuan endeavour to which she applied her wit, intellectualism, grit, determination, creativity, joie de vivre and knowledge to bring to fruition. (Consider the fact that Hurston failed her French-language exit exam on the day of her graduation. She applied herself and retook the exam, receiving her diploma from Barnard in May 1928.) Time and again, Hurston demonstrated over the span of her first three years in New York City her steadfast belief in herself and her work, as well as a commitment to the value and creativity inherent in Black folklore and Black folk cultures. Hurston was a woman on a mission to accomplish the goal of collecting the lore of what she believed was an ever-changing Black folk culture – one shifting due to its proximity to whiteness as well as its distance from its West African roots.

The year 1928 would be Hurston's own, in terms of publications, personal growth and career opportunities. She would travel the expanse of the u.s. southeast over the year, closing it out in New Orleans. This was also the year she would undergo her immersion into voodoo, submitting herself to a 69-hour fast and conversion. Hurston names her initiate as Luke Turner, a Black man at whose pink stucco house she arrived at nine o'clock on a winter morning, and with whom she would spend three days – it would seem for purposes of fieldwork. The moment seems to mark a transformation for Hurston from budding to seasoned scholar. Hurston published her manifesto of selfhood and identity, 'How It Feels to Be Colored Me', in the same year.

During this period, Hurston briefly lived with her husband Herbert Sheen, whom she would later divorce. The two met when undergraduates at Howard in the early 1920s. Photographs of Hurston during this period taken by Sheen, then her college sweetheart, show a Zora who looks far younger than her actual years. The pair shared a mutual admiration for one another, and Hurston was drawn to Sheen's dark skin and good looks. He, like her later loves, reminded her of her loved, longed-for, long-estranged and now deceased father. Sheen gave to Hurston the feeling of family that she had lost after her mother's death in 1904. As Hurston writes in *Dust Tracks on a Road*, 'for the first time since my mother's death, there was someone who felt really close and warm to me.'[1]

Hurston married Sheen, by then a medical student at the University of Chicago, with the expectation and hope that he would provide for her as a husband and that he would not interfere too much with her work. But Hurston was 'assailed with doubts' from the outset.[2] Like Hurston's husbands after Sheen – it is believed that Hurston married on three occasions – Sheen was conflicted about Hurston's devotion to her work. Hurston concluded about her relationship and marriage to Sheen that 'what [she] had taken for eternity turned out to be a moment walking in its sleep.'[3]

Without the success of longevity, Hurston loved, pursued and married Black men she deemed intelligent, handsome and worthy of becoming her husband. All the men were significantly younger than she was and sometimes presented more like disruptive sons than husbands. Jealousy and violence seemed to accrue in Hurston's marital relationships, in time causing their ends. While ongoing, however, these were passionate relationships – both sexually and emotionally – in which Hurston seemed at times to take on a maternal role. In the author notes collected in *Speak, So You Can Speak Again*, Hurston likened herself most to her father in her appreciation for the opposite sex and in her fondness for the many gifts, sexual and otherwise, that men tote. Her husbands, however, required that she choose them rather than her work. For example, within a month of marrying Sheen in St Augustine, Florida, in September 1927, Hurston was bored, feeling constricted and looking for a way out. In a letter of 8 March 1928 to her friend Langston Hughes, Hurston wrote of her decision to end the marriage with Sheen for the reason that 'He tries to hold me back and be generally obtrusive.'[4] Hurston confided to Hughes that she had 'broken off relations since early Jan. and that's that'.[5] The divorce from Sheen was finalized in 1931.

Hurston found her way out through her patron, Mason, whom she met through her friendship with the poet Langston Hughes, and through her association with Alain Locke, a confidante and also a longtime beneficiary of Mason's patronage. Hurston signed a three-year contract with Mason in December 1927. She was now a full-time anthropologist, folklorist and writer, contracted for $200 a month and given a car, a 1928 Chevrolet Coupe. Almost two years later, during the stock market crash of 1929 and through to 1931, Hurston would still be contracted with Mason. This meant that Hurston was sheltered to a degree from the harsh effects and realities of the Great Depression.

When Hurston met Mason, the latter was a lay anthropologist with an interest in what were then thought of as 'primitive' cultures, meaning African American and Native American cultures. Not only was Mason interested in studying these peoples and cultures, she also put her money where her interests lay. In her contract with Mason, Hurston was employed 'to compile and collect information concerning the music, poetry, folk-lore, literature, hoodoo, conjure, manifestations of art and kindred subjects relating to and existing among the North American negroes'.[6] Her assignment was to collect the linguistic, cultural and religious practices and ways of Black Americans. These were the direct descendants of formerly enslaved people, a population that formed a large demographic in the Jim Crow capitalist u.s. South, a place that is still today home to the largest majority of African Americans.

In 1926 Hurston, having transferred to anthropological study, received funding underwritten by a fellowship from

Carter G. Woodson. Hurston collected folklore in the field for the first time during the summer of 1926. She was green, and it showed in her approach. She was also quite busy with writing and collecting data for the reports she was due to submit to Woodson, one of which she plagiarized, perhaps in a rush to complete a requirement of her fellowship. Hurston nevertheless completed her fellowship, and by 1927 she was once again working to access the financial means by which she could continue as a social scientist and collector of folklore. She had travelled throughout the South, including Alabama, New Orleans and her hometown of Eatonville, Florida. She had also spent time at one of her brother's houses in Jacksonville, Florida, in 1927, organizing her research into narratives.

Hurston was funded in her endeavours by white elites primarily, but also Black elites, including Johnson, Locke and Woodson. These were leading African American thinkers; men who would go on to set the pace for their academic disciplines and impact the socio-cultural fabric of the United States through their life and work. Woodson was the second African American in history to receive a degree from Harvard University. W.E.B. Du Bois was the first, in sociology; Locke was the third, in philosophy.

In every instance, whether Hurston's professional relationship was with a Black male member of the elite or with a white elite woman such as Mason, there were dynamics of gender, race, sex and sexuality that needed to be mediated in order for Hurston to live as she wished and to complete her work. Issues of regional difference, social class and caste, including intra-racism and colourism within Black communities, must have impacted these relationships too.

Hurston's time in the field developed her as a researcher and as a woman and thinker. By the time Hurston returned to Eatonville in 1927, she had been away for at least a decade or more, and living in New York for two years. Before that, Hurston had lived first in Baltimore, where she attended Morgan, and then in Washington, DC, while studying at Howard. Hurston had also lived for a year or more in Memphis, Tennessee, and had spent time in Jacksonville and other parts of Florida.

In addition to her salary and the car, Hurston's contract with Mason – who was called 'Godmother' by those she supported, including Hurston – gave her a recording device with which to collect Black folklore. With the financial support of Mason, her well-earned degree and the backing of Franz Boas, Hurston, a Black woman travelling to collect folklore throughout the backwoods of the Jim Crow South, was able to gain hands-on training in her field of research. Significantly, in studying the folk of Eatonville and the town's surrounding areas – people with whom Hurston spent her first and formative years – Hurston was also able to apply the spyglass of anthropology (to invoke her own metaphor in *Mules and Men*) to her own life and circumstances.

It is impossible to say with certainty what the emotional and psychological parameters of Hurston's relationships with her white female benefactors were, except that 'white women played . . . an outsized . . . role in Hurston's professional life – mediating her access to economic and intellectual resources'.[7] These financial, professional, personal and at times emotionally intimate relationships required of Hurston her time, intelligence and candour – as well as her willingness to dissemble and variously play the part of a child or a sycophant. Hurston's contract with

Hurston in the driver's seat of an automobile, *c.* 1928/9.

Hurston, *c.* 1920s or early 1930s, wearing a beret. Hurston indicates in her 1928 essay 'How It Feels to Be Colored Me' her preference for a hat tipped to the side. A fashionable French beret seems appropriate for a cosmopolitan woman such as Hurston.

Mason officially ended in December 1931; Hurston would turn 41 the following January. Just three years later, without the financial support – and creative restraint – of Mason, Hurston published her first novel, *Jonah's Gourd Vine*. Her contract with Lippincott, a major white publisher, came with a $200 advance, much of which was used to pay rent on the home that Hurston was living in at the time.

Hurston published 'How It Feels to Be Colored Me' despite being under contract with Mason, who could be mercurial and who 'believed herself to be a "better Negro" . . . than most of the African Americans she knew'.[8] In fact, as Mason wrote 'in a letter to Locke', she considered herself to be 'a Black God in African art compared to you in the nourishment I give the Negroes, from the root of their primitive ancestry'.[9] Paranoid, and concerned about being exploited by her African American clients, Mason 'constantly worried she was being taken advantage of' and as such 'kept insinuating that [Hurston] was being extravagant, and [thus] continually reminded her of the terms of her contract'.[10] Hurston had to submit to questions by Mason such as 'Why couldn't Negroes be trusted?'[11]

So when Hurston published 'How It Feels to Be Colored Me', she did so in full knowledge of possible blowback from Mason. Their contract stipulated 'ownership of collected material to Mason' and forbade Hurston 'to make material known to anyone not designated in writing by Mason'.[12] Hurston was, as always, short on cash and had debts like any striving artist. She published 'How It Feels to Be Colored Me' despite such contractual constraints. Hurston was in effect showcasing for readers, as well as perhaps for Mason, the 'New Negro', herself – a Black, modern female subject whose freedom was a given since it was paid for, in full, by her formerly enslaved ancestors. By its very existence, then, 'How It Feels to Be Colored Me' is an assertion by Hurston of her personal freedom. Perhaps understandably, particularly as a direct descendant of formerly enslaved African Americans, Hurston rebuffed attempts to truncate or in any way foreclose her life and work. When she published the essay – which she did in a popular publication rather than an academic one – she was already a published researcher who had completed fieldwork and written reports, including articles for

Woodson and Boas, pre-eminent in their respective fields of history and anthropology. In penning 'How It Feels to Be Colored Me', Hurston introduced herself to the world as a writer of ethnographic and by turns creative non-fiction.

In the essay, Hurston renders herself a modern American subject who feels 'most colored' in all-white spaces, especially elite ones such as Barnard College. Hurston invokes and amends her mentor Locke's concept of the New Negro, introduced in 1925, by rendering the New Negro a Black woman with erudition and a healthy sense of her own personhood and self-worth. The New Negro is cosmopolitan, a mobile subject who (to the degree possible considering the epoch) can outmatch even leading white aristocrats of the day. This is another way of saying that Hurston exceeds the standard when in her element. In fact, in 'How It Feels to Be Colored Me', she is the standard.

Hurston's essay displays a new image and idea of Black womanhood and Black women's subjectivity. This was a time when the common conception of Black women in mainstream white (and, too often, African American) society and culture was as dirty in bodily, spiritual and sexual ways. Hurston also demonstrates in the essay and through her own self-fashioning the temporal and spatial location of the early twentieth-century Black woman, which she suggests is both fixed and shifting.

Curiosity compels 'cosmic Zora', as Hurston conceives of herself in 'How It Feels to Be Colored Me', just as it compelled 'everybody's Zora' in Eatonville when she was a child.[13] Curiosity is the vehicle by which Hurston took heed of her mother's advice and jumped at the sun.[14] Hurston did more than get off the ground, as her beloved mother must have known she would. She became a collector and creator of both a culture and a people; the progenitor and continuation of an intellectual legacy of Black thought in the United States. She taught herself what she did not know, and learned from and among the best and brightest minds of a people, a generation and a nation. She was more than a contender; she was, to paraphrase Kentucky's champion Muhammad Ali, one of the greatest.

Hurston opens 'How It Feels to Be Colored Me' by stating, 'I am colored but I offer nothing in the way of extenuating circumstances except the fact that I am the only Negro in the United States whose grandfather on the mother's side was *not* an Indian chief.' Hurston continues, 'I remember the very day that I became colored.'[15] What is extraordinary is Hurston's suggestion of her willingness to accept herself as is and without need of apology or qualification. The essay posits: how do you exist as 'colored' in a national landscape that kept generations of your family enslaved, and illiterate, by legal means, for centuries? How does it feel not simply to be coloured, Hurston provides, but to be 'colored me'? Here, Hurston writes the individual and the collective. In addition to being African American, she is a woman, one born into government-sanctioned generational poverty – a poverty that generations of her family, especially her parents and grandparents, worked diligently to escape.

Central to 'How It Feels to Be Colored Me' is music, in particular the relatively new African American genre jazz, a music form that 'constricts the thorax and splits the heart with its tempo and narcotic harmonies'.[16] Hurston writes of being compelled by the drumbeat and rhythm of African American music, which for her transcends geographic distances and differences and resituates her in her West and Central African ancestral lands: 'I dance wildly inside myself; I yell within, I whoop; I shake my assegai above my head, I hurl it true to the mark *yeeeeooww!*'[17] Hurston hears jazz and sees colours in the same way that, when she was in high school at the age of 26, she heard her African American teacher read Coleridge's 'Kubla Khan' for the first time. Music, words, poetry and beauty move Hurston to see, and often to act. Music, like poetry, allowed her the opportunity to escape the moment. This too is how Hurston knows her difference. Music, particularly jazz, is one of the ways that she knows and feels her colour, which is to say, how it feels to be who she is.

According to the Hurston scholar Carla Kaplan, Mason never forgot the 'minutiae of [her clients'] daily lives . . . interesting herself in every detail of their struggles'.[18] For example, Yuval Taylor adds that Mason required Hurston to keep and provide records of 'all things financial, domestic, nutritional, and digestive . . . every penny spent, every piece of linen purchased, every calorie consumed, each bodily waste emitted'.[19] In a perhaps jocular statement as to Mason's motivations, Taylor, quoting Kaplan, writes of Mason, 'She *craved* people. She lived for the moments when she could see into someone's soul and divine just how his or her life should be lived.'[20] Hurston felt demoralized often in her relationship with Mason; she confessed in a letter to Hughes that her patron sometimes 'destroys my self-respect . . . and utterly demoralizes me for weeks . . . I can't endure to get at odds with her.'[21] Mason seemed to regard herself as a figurative mother to figurative children, and she might have seen her guidance of them as a gift. Mason wrote in a letter to a friend in 1923, prior to meeting Hurston: 'That is the reward of being a godmother, to share the ecstasy of first moments with her children.'[22]

Early on in their contractual relationship, Hurston would discover that Mason, the 'short, elderly, white-haired, beautifully dressed white woman', was in fact 'a jealous god, controlling and wrathful'.[23] Fundamentally, Mason 'believed that American Negroes and Indians were "younger races unspoiled by white civilization", whose primitive creativity and spirituality would energize and renew America'.[24] Mason was not alone in her thoughts – we might think of the popularity of primitivism, 'the cure-all for the ills of civilization', as an artistic and cultural movement in the United States and Europe in the late nineteenth and early twentieth centuries.[25] This was the intellectual, political, sociocultural and personal framework in which Hurston and Mason met, engaged and together constructed both Zora Neale Hurston as an anthropologist and folklorist and *Mules and Men*, the folklore collection that would result from their contractual relationship.

Taylor's *Godfather* reference points to the certain challenge for Hurston in fostering and maintaining this important relationship in her life. Taylor goes further to read a desire for influence on a world level in Mason's patronage, and writes that Mason paid her patrons 'lavishly' as a means of controlling 'their output'.[26] Such control, ensured by Mason's financial and personal influence, allowed for the advancement of Mason's 'pet cause . . . the idea of the American Negro as the archetypal primitive, a bridge to an uncorrupted world'.[27] Her 'fondest hope was to make a difference to the world through mystical connection to the primitive, which would overwhelm the malign forces of civilization'.[28] Many who met Mason regarded her as something of a 'goddess'.[29] Taylor writes of Mason's patrons as 'acolytes' who held the elite white woman and lay anthropologist in high regard. In fact, as Taylor writes, Hurston 'was given to flattery in her letters, but her worshipful missives to Mason read as if they had been addressed to a pagan idol'.[30] Taylor quotes a letter to Mason in which Hurston, less than two years into her contract, writes, 'It is you who gives out life and light and we who receive,' adding further effusive language suggestive of a relationship to a god and not a mortal being.[31] Hurston was surely exercising her right as both a writer and a storyteller to construct an image of herself and her relationship with Mason that would surely flatter Mason. Hurston was probably also telling truths, no matter how slant. Mason provided her with economic support for three years of her adult life. Many other researchers would have leapt at such an opportunity. As Taylor further notes, 'this devotion wasn't just what Mason inspired – it was what she demanded.'[32] Hurston had to court Mason and her financial support continuously, and often by any means necessary.

The wear on Hurston is evidenced in her letters. As Mary Helen Washington writes, Hurston was 'hard pressed for money for her [whole] career'.[33] Further, she

> needed to travel to the South to spend time with people who knew the folk stories [she wished to collect] and would tell them only to trusted friends. Few black scholars had the kind of money to finance such an expedition. But even the contract with Mrs Mason did not relieve Hurston of money worries. At one time she had to itemise her expenses for Mrs Mason to show how she was handling the money. She had to account for such obvious necessities as shoe repair, car fare, and medicine; even a box of Kotex is listed. Once or twice she mentions the intestinal

problem that was beginning to trouble her, in order to justify buying medication for treatment.[34]

From 1928 until their contracted work ended in 1931, Mason would fund – with upwards of $15,000 – and by extension control in large part Hurston's research and life. Theirs, at least for a time, was a relationship of mutuality. Hurston wanted to conduct research and ultimately to write about what she suggests was an indigenous African American life and culture, relatively unspoiled by association with and acculturation among white Americans – that is, the culture of Eatonville, the rural, labouring-class African American community in which she was raised and came to consciousness as a Black girl.

Hurston was 37 years old in 1928, the year she contracted with Mason and graduated from Barnard, and though she was often fearful of being found out by Mason and sometimes paralysed by her fear of the woman's power, Hurston generally did share her collected material with confidants she deemed trustworthy, including the writers Langston Hughes and Dorothy West – and with readers of *World Tomorrow*, an early twentieth-century periodical that was then and for a short time under the editorship of Hurston's fellow Harlem Renaissance writer and novelist Wallace Thurman. While Hurston was critical of Mason in private letters, at one time suggesting that she was wearing down her spirit, she 'never publicly discussed' Mason's 'paternalism, her racism'.[35]

The contractual link between Hurston and Mason also necessitated Hurston's performed intellectual and personal subordination to Mason. In a letter of 16 April 1930 to her former professor and mentor Boas, Hurston writes of being summoned to Mason's Park Avenue apartment – which Hurston refers to as her headquarters – with the command that Hurston 'come over Friday at three, and bring materials for discussion'.[36] Hurston adds, 'I suppose it is merely intended to see how I am doing . . . I am urged to do things as quickly as possible and so at present am working furiously.'[37] (According to Taylor, Mason's home at 399 Park Avenue was a 'twelve-room apartment'.[38]) The requested 'materials' were most likely the folklore Hurston had collected in the southeastern United States, which consisted of 'the music, poetry, folk-lore, literature, hoodoo, conjure, [and other] manifestations of art and kindred subjects relating to and existing among the North American negroes.'[39] This was the folklore that would later make up *Mules and Men.*

And yet one month and two days later, in an aforementioned letter – the occasion of which was Mason's 76th birthday – Hurston wrote to Mason celebrating her birth, her contributions, her life and years. The letter is exuberant and exceedingly fawning, containing the implication that Mason is not only a literal life-saver for Hurston and untold others but that she is a demigod of sorts, with inestimable qualities. Hurston writes of Mason's birthday as a renewal of her 'promise to the world to shine and brill for another year', and of Mason as 'God's flower, and my flower . . . and the world's blossom'.[40] In the letter, Hurston writes of herself as being 'one of the rescued', who thanks to Mason was 'dragged from everlasting unseeing to heaven!' She concludes with the wish for the promise of 'another year' of being 'bless[ed]' by Mason's presence and, by association, her economic championing and support.[41] A sketch by Hurston at the top of the letter features images of peaks and valleys, what look like hieroglyphs and a sun rising or setting beyond a mountain range; the words 'love', 'wisdom' and 'creation' are written in capitals, with Hurston seemingly attributing these traits to her patron.[42]

Mason was a white woman from the American elite whose wealth was such that even though she lost 50 per cent of her fortune during the stock market crash of 1929 and the Great Depression that followed, this staggering loss of wealth barely marred her position. She was able to maintain her opulent lifestyle. This was with one exception, however: as with other white benefactors whose monies served to underwrite the literary and cultural phenomenon that was the Harlem Renaissance of the 1920s, Mason was less inclined to fund artists during and following the Depression.

Hurston's three-year contract with Mason saw Hurston collect, document, record and render in writing the musical, religious, cultural and everyday traditions of labouring-class Black people –

Hurston in Eatonville, Florida, June 1935, with the musicians Rochelle French and Gabriel Brown.

that is, those masses of largely uneducated, working people living in the South whom W.E.B. Du Bois dubbed 'the folk' in his groundbreaking work *The Souls of Black Folk* (1903).

When Mason and Hurston met, Hurston was in her late thirties and Mason was in her seventies and widowed. In 1928 Hurston was six years shy of seeing the publication of her first novel. Although under contract with Mason, she was strapped for cash. This was not an unusual predicament for a self-made, full-time writer and researcher. She was, moreover, a Black woman alone in the world: newly single but not yet divorced and without the support – particularly economic – of a spouse. Hurston did marry again, and by most standards she married well. While her husbands were not well off, they were educated and upwardly mobile, like her. Also like Hurston, they were high achievers in pursuit of all things deemed relevant to the American Dream, the economic and professional success that would beget them a family, a home and some pleasures, even within Jim Crow society. Hurston's three husbands were Harry

Hurston on a boat rowed by an African American man, conducting fieldwork and collecting folklore on behalf of the anthropologist Jane Belo, *c.* 1935–9.

Hurston and an unidentified man in Belle Glade, Florida, probably at a recording site, *c.* 1936.

Sheen (1927–31), Albert Price (1939–43) and James Howell Pitts (18 January–31 October 1944). However, Hurston, older by at least a decade than all three, could not make it work with her younger husbands. She chose her career at a time when it was standard practice for a woman to limit herself to marriage and mothering. Hurston was willing to marry, it seems, but there was never any mention on her part of a desire to be a mother or a traditional wife. What she wanted most was to establish herself as a writer and to find success in her work. In the summer of 1928, only a few months before she would separate from her first husband, Hurston drafted and saw published 'How It Feels to Be Colored Me'.

It may be instructive to consider why this short essay was written and published. The scholar Adrienne Brown situates Hurston's canonical essay alongside the British modernist Virginia Woolf's famous work 'A Room of One's Own' (1929), in which Woolf famously argued that women need a 'room of one's own' in order to create art that is of value, and thus lasting. Brown writes that, although it was published a year earlier, Hurston's essay has not been thought of in the critical scholarship as 'groundbreaking' in the way that Woolf's has, and that it might rightly be read 'as a treatise on the conditions of Black women's writing' and thus shares 'a genre with "A Room of One's Own"'.[43] Brown reads Hurston's essay as describing the 'value' Hurston 'finds in continually making herself public, of putting her body out in the world and on the line'.[44] Brown argues that this self-positioning by Hurston began when she was a child in Eatonville and performed and danced for white Northern travellers passing through the then unpaved one-road town. Hurston remembered the reactions to her impishness, when she would engage with the white strangers on their travels: 'Usually [the] automobile or the horse paused . . . and after a queer exchange of compliments, I would probably "go a piece of the way" with them, as we say in the farthest Florida.'[45] Hurston adds, 'They liked to hear me "speak pieces" and sing and wanted to see me dance the parse-me-la, and gave generously of their small silver for doing these things, which seemed strange to me for I wanted to do them so much that I needed bribing to stop.'[46] Hurston, knowingly as a woman and unknowingly as a girl, rendered herself a spectacle for the white passers-by, according to Brown. Zora's actions were both feared and rejected by her community in her childhood, and perhaps too in her adulthood. Brown says, however, that such positioning on Hurston's part became a way for the girl (and woman) to exercise her ability to tell stories and play, and in effect to gain an early and self-directed autonomy, even in the midst of community criticism, backlash, outright resistance and fear. In her reading of Hurston's famous essay, Brown suggests that this accessing of autonomy for Zora the young girl was mutually satisfying: as Hurston writes in 'How It Feels to Be Colored Me', she got as much pleasure (and sometimes a dime) out of performing as her white audience did from the performance.[47]

In telling the story of who she is, and offering her perspective on white and Black American life and culture, Hurston functions in the essay as both a cultural critic and an early African American memoirist. We may think here of the work Alice Walker does in her 1983 essay 'Beauty: When the Other Dancer Is the Self': the kind of self-reflection and self-revelation that we see in Walker's essay (as well as in Woolf's, for that matter) is modelled earlier in 'How It Feels to Be Colored Me', in which Hurston simultaneously crafts and presents her own Black female modernist subjectivity as a New Negro. In doing so, she engages with, and furthers, the cultural concept introduced three years earlier by her former mentor Locke. Hurston also writes herself as a modernist subject, and in particular as a modern American subject, in effect establishing herself as a new voice of twentieth-century American and African American creative and intellectual thought. Through embodiment and self-fashioning in the essay, Hurston centres and re-genders the New Negro as a woman who transcends class, if not caste, and as an intellectual.

The preoccupations of the woman authoring the essay are the ways in which family, culture, gender, nation, race and historical time, as well as historical legacies, inform not only our experiences of but our ideas about selfhood, identity, nation and more. Hurston establishes in the essay that primary for her is to not *feel* her race – that is, to simply be herself, to be 'cosmic' and not limited or circumscribed by race and racism (among other factors), to understand herself beautifully as 'me', in all the complexity that concept entails.

For Hurston, then, it is the absence of Black people and Black community and her isolation among white people and white community that renders her coloured. Hurston writes, 'I do not always feel colored . . . Even now I often achieve the unconscious Zora of Eatonville before the Hegira.' She writes that she feels 'most colored . . . when I am thrown against a sharp white background. For instance at Barnard.'[48] Racial isolation for a self-conceived cosmic soul born with a spirit of curiosity and a vast imagination, who learned and harnessed reading comprehension when young, is a limitation. It is the absence of kin and kind, Hurston suggests, that renders her 'thrown', and thus destabilized. Racial isolation, then, is murderous for Hurston as a creative and as an intellectual. So too is cultural isolation, as well as economic disenfranchisement for her as a Black woman creative, intellectual and artist.

In 'How It Feels to Be Colored Me', Hurston writes with assurance that she is 'not tragically colored'. Further, she posits that humans are perhaps no more than 'brown bag[s] of miscellany' and, by suggestion, that the God of Christian theology is but a 'Great Stuffer of Bags', indifferent to the simultaneously priceless and worthless trinkets that go into stuffing them – that is, creating humans.[49] Hurston's essay challenges notions of humanity, African American subjectivity and Black womanhood. In questioning the inherited ideas and beliefs endemic to American and African American life and culture, Hurston instead offers, and thus privileges, her own suppositions regarding the images and ideas of these subjects. Are readers to take the adult Hurston, the university trained, award-winning and published social scientist and writer, at her word? Are we to believe that even as an adult Hurston still regarded her home community's response to her childhood performances as unfavourable (for little reason other than they hated seeing a person, perhaps especially a girl, have a good time)? Is this Hurston a trickster at work? What is the relevance of telling this story? One can say it is a child's wisdom remembered through the lens of an adult woman. Hurston is telling her readers specific things about herself: first, she was born for the stage (that is, the world) and made for the performance engendered by the white passers-by; and second, she had been on the move, both literally and metaphorically, and had attracted the attention of voyeuristic, moneyed and legally and culturally powerful white others (including her readers and her patrons) from a very young age.

Brown writes that Hurston's essay highlights 'moments when she relinquished control over her space, body, and art – sometimes with pleasure, sometimes with great pain – to place herself, often literally, in the path of white women who were her most regular patrons'.[50] Hurston, according to Brown, doubles down on depicting positive moments of herself in public (for example, on a walk in New York City or in a clubroom listening to a jazz ensemble) as well as in her childhood performances in front of her family's home. The question becomes, then, why? Why would Hurston feel the need to project a positive image of herself when she was now an educated Black woman and sophisticate in a Northern, urban and clearly classist space such as New York City? Perhaps, as Brown suggests, it was to jettison, subvert or challenge prevailing ideas about and images of Black women in the larger culture. Hurston writes herself as whole, alert, alive and free when in public in New York ('I set my hat at a certain angle and saunter down Seventh Avenue, Harlem City, feeling as snooty as the lions in front of the Forty-Second Street Library'[51]). It seems that geographic location impacts not only how she conceives of herself but her experience of herself.

Hurston, despite all obstacles, was a Black American woman with a voice, presence, style, pedigree – and a platform. She suggests by way of 'How It Feels to Be Colored Me' that there is a full acceptance of her Black woman self despite how others regarded her. Hurston goes further by establishing distance between herself and what she suggests is contemporary status quo Blackness: the accepted subordination to whiteness or Europeanism. She also distinguished herself from what she suggests is an almost innate lack of culture and feeling, a coldness, within contemporaneous white American society as well as within aspects of contemporaneous Black American society – the latter represented by those unnamed Eatonville inhabitants who 'deplored any joyful tendencies in me'.[52]

At the moment of the essay's publication in 1928, the African American music form of jazz was relatively new to audiences. As a way of foregrounding her difference, as well as foregrounding Black music, Hurston writes in 'How It Feels to Be Colored Me' of a time when she and a white male stranger shared a table at a cabaret and sat listening to a jazz band. Hurston was immediately drawn in by the music. The white man, however, seemed unmoved by the same music that so enlivened Hurston and made her feel as if her 'pulse [was] a throbbing war drum'.[53] Through this scene, Hurston shows that the pair's difference is cultural and, to a degree, intuitive. She implies that African Americans such as herself are different and respond differently to cultural presentations representative of Black American culture. Hurston – an African-descended, Black American elite woman – shakes her 'assegai above [her] head'.[54] On the inside, at least, she reverts to her pagan self, which is not a reduced self but rather one in hiding, or perhaps shielded, from the veneer of white civilization. The white man in her essay is, with the exception of a finger tap or three, ostensibly immune to the visceral, emotive, musical and imaginative sway of jazz music that Hurston is so alive to. Hurston, by contrast, is an impassioned, embodied receptor of the music. She is a savage self torn free from the confines of the white society and culture that has diminished her.

The suggestion in the essay is that jazz allows for the engagement of Hurston's anima. Whereas the white man sits motionless, drumming his fingers to the music, only to say, simply, 'Good music they have here,' Hurston is enthralled by the sounds coming from the band.[55] 'Smoking calmly', the white man – a synecdoche for civilization and for whiteness itself – is unaware of the energy stirring mere inches away in the woman seated beside him.[56] Hurston is floored by his stillness. The music, which moves her profoundly, seems barely to have touched the white listener. The 'great blobs of purple and red emotion' that grip Hurston merely entertain her tablemate.[57] The white male listener seems only to hear, while Hurston both hears and feels. This contrast between the two audience members compounds the already significant differences the author suggests exist between them. A metaphoric ocean emerges between subjects, and Hurston can see for herself their difference, writing, 'he is so pale with his whiteness then and I am so colored.'[58]

Significantly, it is in New York City, in 1928, while walking alone, dressed up, hat donned, along Seventh Avenue in Harlem, that Hurston feels, as she writes, like 'me'. What is the 'self' Hurston introduces to readers in this essay? What image of the New Negro emerges? Hurston presents herself as a woman who, through years of association with white Americans, as well as in the context of her own Southern Black community, is accustomed to constant misunderstanding, resistance and, she suggests, otherwise passionless white Americans or groups of fervently emotional Black Americans. Hurston's essay is a rejection of all that both races and cultures can offer to her. She instead seeks to foster a space in which she, a self-loving and self-governing Black elite woman (albeit without means), can exist as herself. Hurston juxtaposes her own version of Blackness with that of the Eatonville community of her childhood. While she is not 'tragically colored', as she writes in the essay, some of her townspeople are. She juxtaposes her own Blackness, and Americanness, with that of the staid white male listener, and the larger white society of which he is representative.

Hurston, as her writing states, was different. It was not just Eatonville Black people from whom Hurston suggested she was dissimilar, but the majority of Black Americans. She had and carried within herself pride and dignity, meaning she had no need to engender claims to be anything more or less than she was. 'How It Feels to Be Colored Me' is a powerful if subtle critique of Anglophilia, intra-racism and internalized self-hate within Black communities, and a rejection of what Hurston seemed to regard as the staid and passionless society and culture of contemporaneous white America and white American womanhood. Race hate, internalized and transferred, Hurston suggested, is an ill of Black

America. For her, however, being Black or 'colored', to use the language of the essay and of the times, was but a fact of her identity and means something only in the context of white spaces, the white images and celebrities of the culture and, ultimately, a white supremacist, apartheid nation. Hurston drew on what the feminist scholar Jane Gallop in the 1990s has since termed 'anecdotal theory' to deliver a slew of lessons about how she saw and experienced, and discursively produced and reproduced, her life and the world of u.s. society and culture.

Hurston was a nomad from birth, it seems, and perhaps primed for her work as a folklorist, anthropologist and, ultimately, novelist. Born in Alabama and relocating to Florida, a state she would forever claim as her place of birth, Hurston began life in transit. When her mother died in 1904 and Hurston's father sent her away to Jacksonville to attend a Christian boarding school, abandoning his daughter soon after, Hurston's transitory life was set in motion. Years later, in 1928, Hurston became a studious researcher. The creative and intellectual work that came out of what was an industrious and fast-moving time in Hurston's life continues to inform her legacy.

4

On Fiction and Folklore

In April 1932, low on funds and working on the manuscript for *Mules and Men*, Hurston made the decision to return to Florida. There she would be able to live more cheaply than in New York and perhaps gain a bit of distance from the city, and from her former employer, Charlotte Osgood Mason. Mason 'grudgingly gave [Hurston] six dollars for a new pair of shoes, enough cash for a one-way ticket to Eatonville, and seventy-five dollars for the road'.[1]

By 1932, Hurston had achieved a lot. She had a college education at a time when few Americans, regardless of race, could claim the same, and she belonged to the vanguard of writers who would come to represent the Harlem Renaissance. Hurston had also had several long- and short-term careers in domestic service under her belt and was well connected both through this work and as a result of her own intelligence or, in her words, 'impertinence'; she had managed to care and provide for herself from the age of fourteen. Hurston had shared a deep and abiding, although ultimately troubled, relationship with her fellow writer and poet Langston Hughes, and had been contracted to work full-time as a researcher for Mason, a wealthy white woman benefactor with whom she felt she had a spiritual bond. Hurston had also written and produced a series of dramatic productions developed from folklore collected while in the service of Mason. One such production was *The Great Day* in 1932. which Hurston wrote, produced and acted in, and which achieved some minor success in New York. But the assistance from Mason left her indebted.

The woman returning home to Eatonville for a sojourn was not the girl who left Eatonville at fourteen in search of a better life.

Hurston performing a scene from her play *The Great Day.* Hurston often wrote, produced and acted in her own productions.

Hurston had largely found and made that life for herself, although she had the help of her siblings, and in particular her only sister, Sarah Hurston Mack, and their older brother, John, both of whom provided housing for Hurston at different times in her early adulthood. It is significant that she had the patronage of a handful of elite white women, people whom she needed in order to break free from the material poverty and requisite lack of access that circumscribed her life.

Hurston's letters from the period reflect a woman on the verge of a breakthrough. But Hurston did not yet know it, for that spring she was at a personal nadir following the death of her sister Sarah, a woman who had named her only child, a daughter, after Zora. Sarah was 43 years old, according to Valerie Boyd's *Wrapped in Rainbows* (2003), and Zora was 42. Hurston wrote in a 20 March 1933 letter to Alain Locke, 'My sister died very recently in New Jersey . . . I am hard hit.' Hurston must have discovered in herself a renewed determination to make her desires and dreams a reality, and in quick order. She had already lost her mother and father and now was mourning the loss of her beloved older sister.

As Robert Hemenway notes, Hurston 'had been writing furiously' in the years prior to her return to the South. In 1931 she finished writing *Barracoon: The Story of the Last 'Black Cargo'*, a recount of her 1927 folklore expedition to Plateau, Alabama, to interview 86-year-old Cudjoe Lewis, an African man who, at nineteen years old, survived the *Clotilda*, which was the last known slave ship to make the translantic passage, transporting Africans into slavery. The work was not published in Hurston's lifetime. Instead, *Barracoon* was

Hurston at a Federal Writers' Project exhibit in 1938, reading a book entitled *American Stuff*.

published posthumously in 2018 and edited by the scholar Deborah G. Plant with a foreword by Alice Walker. Hemenway continues that Hurston 'wrote sketches for two theatrical revues, published the long essay "Hoodoo in America" in the *Journal of American Folklore*, and wrote and organised a folk concert called *The Great Day*.'[2] Also, in 1933 she wrote her first novel, *Jonah's Gourd Vine*, and revised *Mules and Men*, which was published in 1935 with a foreword by Franz Boas. 'Both were published by Lippincott, a major publisher, and were very well received in the mainstream press.'[3] The novel *Their Eyes Were Watching God*, Hurston's 'masterpiece', followed, written in 1936 'in the space of seven weeks' and published the following year.[4] Yuval Taylor notes that this novel 'remains the single most widely read book ever written by an African American'.[5] It continues to outsell works such as Ralph Ellison's *Invisible Man* (1952), Maya Angelou's *I Know Why the Caged Bird Sings* (1969) and Alice Walker's *The Color Purple* (1982). Beverly Guy-Sheftall writes that *Their Eyes Were Watching God* 'underscored the importance [to Black women of] finding their own voices and liberating themselves from narrow conceptions of womanhood'.[6]

In 1934, Hurston's essay on Black art and Black aesthetics, 'Characteristics of Negro Expression', was published in the British writer and activist Nancy Cunard's edited collection *Negro Anthology*. In this now canonical essay, Hurston collected and codified what she conceived of as characteristics of contemporaneous Black folk peoples, such as 'Angularity'.

> A striking manifestation of the Negro is Angularity. Everything that he touches becomes angular. In all African sculpture and doctrine of any sort we find the same thing. Anyone watching Negro dancers will be struck by the same phenomenon. Every posture is another angle. Pleasing, yes. But an effect achieved by the very means which an European strives to avoid. The pictures on the walls are hung at deep angles. Furniture is always set at an angle. I have instances of a piece of furniture in the middle of a wall being set with one end nearer the wall than the other to avoid the simple straight line.[7]

Such characteristics of angularity also include the will to adorn or beautify and, famously, as Hurston argues, the impulse towards mimicry. These characteristics can be evidenced in the creation of the new in art, life and culture, such as jazz and Blues, according to Hurston. Hurston's essay is a forerunner of the work of the critic Addison Gayle Jr and his groundbreaking anthology *The Black Aesthetic* (1970).

Hurston applied for and was granted two Guggenheim Fellowships in her lifetime, the first in 1936 and the second in 1937. With the first grant, she was able to complete her second novel, *Their Eyes Were Watching God*, and with the second she began work on her second folklore collection, *Tell My Horse* (1938). The work Hurston did in the 1930s was influenced by the disciplines of anthropology, folklore, literature and more, along with her ongoing and driving desire to capture and codify African American folk life and culture.

Jonah's Gourd Vine and *Mules and Men* not only reflect Hurston's style as a writer but, notably, showcase her modernist sensibility, identifiable in Hurston's subject-matter, language, use of dialogue and in the very structure of the works themselves. Hurston uses both Standard English and African American Vernacular English (AAVE), also referred to as Black English, in both works. While other writers such as the poet Paul Laurence Dunbar stuck to one language form, in Dunbar's case Black or Plantation English, Hurston, a modernist subject whose writing was published some twenty or more years after Dunbar's, combines multiple language types. She also employed third-person narration in works and played around with structure.

In her first novel, Hurston borrowed from her parents' early courtship and marriage. In her first folklore collection, Hurston used literary tropes such as foreshadowing, narrative, setting, dialogue and characterization as means of rendering her scholarly research more interesting for and accessible to a lay reading audience. She also did this, I suggest, because it was part of her aesthetic and style – this blending is suggestive of the woman herself, a woman who straddled eras (Victorian and nineteenth

Hurston in 1934, the year her first novel, *Jonah's Gourd Vine*, was published.

and twentieth centuries) as well as countries (antebellum and postbellum America). This blending is also suggestive of the people she studied and wrote about, those she made her subjects, whose very survival depended on their ability to straddle actual and figurative worlds as Black American subjects in a former, and actual, slavocracy. Hurston identified as a Negro, and, more to the point, she saw no lack within Black culture that was endemic or specific to it, instead regarding any lack as being within what she identified as the 'imaginative wasteland of white society'.[8]

With regard to the meaning behind the title of *Jonah's Gourd Vine*, Hurston wrote to her long-time friend the white writer and cultural critic-turned-photographer Carl Van Vechten on 28 February 1934 to explain it (clearly, he had not comprehended the meaning, as she wrote, 'Oh yes, the title you didn't understand'[9]).

Hurston points Van Vechten to the biblical figure of Jonah, and in particular to Chapter 4, verses 6–10 of the Book of Jonah. She wrote, 'You see the prophet of God sat up under a gourd vine that had grown up in one night. But a cut worm came along and cut it down.' She explained: 'Great and sudden growth. One act of malice and it is withered and gone.'[10] Here Hurston could be referencing the actions of her ostensibly democratic home nation, and even those of her father towards her mother when she was alive – the main character, John Pearson, has a wife called Lucy, the name of Hurston's mother.

Hurston's return to Eatonville in 1932 might have suggested a low point in her life and career, but it was also a new beginning for the writer and novelist. Hurston went to work codifying Black American folk life, including its language, work and work songs, sex, romantic love and marriage, politics, arts, sexual politics and religions. As well as fieldwork and published folklore, she did this through theatrical productions, short stories such as 'The Gilded Six-Bits' (1933), published in *Story* magazine, and by which she gained the notice of publishers in northern states. Hurston's autobiography, *Dust Tracks on a Road*, and, ultimately, her novels (the ones discussed as well as *Moses, Man of the Mountain* (1939) and *Seraph on the Suwanee* (1948)) also function as ways of codifying imaginative aspects of the Black experience, for contemporaneous and for future audiences.

Hurston saw value in the people and cultures she studied and imagined. Hurston never left her subject, even as she shifted in matters of character and characterization. All her novels foreground family dynamics, especially their sexual politics – whether the character is a Black American, as they most often are, or a white American, such as in *Seraph on the Suwanee*.

As Mary Helen Washington writes, the 1930s marked the 'meridian of Hurston's career'.[11] Hurston's publications during this decade demonstrate her move 'to take her work in directions that would earn her both high praise and severe censure'.[12] Washington explains that 'in an era when many educated and cultured blacks prided themselves on removing all traces of their rural black origins, when a high-class "Negro" virtue was not to "act one's color," Hurston did what some saw as the very opposite.'[13]

Washington writes, 'Zora not only celebrated the distinctivenss of black culture, but saw those traditional black folkways as marked improvements' over white society, the imagination of which Hurston found to be deficient.[14] Hurston also saw fault within Black folk culture, but specifically within how Black society and culture aped that of white people.

Hurston was able to secure a contract from Lippincott for her first folklore collection – part of a three-book deal Hurston signed with the publisher in 1933–4. As with the writing of her second and signature novel, *Their Eyes Were Watching God*, Hurston wrote *Jonah's Gourd Vine* in a matter of months. She completed her work in Florida and then returned to New York to live and work in the city in 1935. Hurston achieved all of this without funding from Mason. She had fostered friendships with well-placed professors and administrators at the all-white Rollins College in Orange County, Florida, and with their help Hurston staged an updated version of her play *The Great Day*, retitled *From Sun to Sun* (1932). It was Robert Wunsch, a professor in the English department at Rollins, who sent Hurston's short story 'The Gilded Six-Bits' to *Story* magazine, and it was the college's then president, Hamilton Holt, and another professor in the English department there, Edwin O. Grover, who invited Hurston to visit the campus. Hurston and Grover would remain in contact via letters for a decade or more after meeting. With the publication of 'The Gilded Six-Bits' in *Story*, which garnered Hurston a larger, Northern white readership, Hurston had secured a publisher, a book contract and seen the publication of one of her now much-anthologized short stories in an elite publication. During this time in Florida, Hurston made and established connections, friendships and alliances, a pattern that she continued in New York, including with the legendary stage performer and blues singer Ethel Waters ('She is shy and you must convince her that she is really wanted before she will open up her tender parts and show you'[15]).

Hurston was chided by a friend, Harry Block, for signing with J. B. Lippincott for her first novel; Block apparently thought Hurston rated higher, especially considering Lippincott's primary focus was textbook publishing. Hurston confided in a letter of 31 January 1935 to the Mexican artist Miguel Covarrubias, who illustrated Hurston's *Mules and Men*, 'but you see, I had a bid from [Lippincott] before *Jonah's Gourd Vine* was even written and you know a bird in the hand is worth a whole covey up a tree.'[16]

Hurston was 43 years old when she secured the book contract for *Jonah's Gourd Vine*; the book was published the following year. It was the first of four novels Hurston would publish; the first three with Lippincott and the fourth with Scribner's. Hurston had been considering the idea for *Jonah's Gourd Vine* for three or four years before she sat down to capture the life and story of John Pearson, a free Black man born to an enslaved Black mother.

The rape of Black women during slavery is central to the novel. John Pearson, Hurston suggests – that is, she foregrounds it without showcasing it – is the child of rape. His mother, Amy Crittenden, was assaulted by her white master, Alf, whom we learn is John's biological father and of whom John is the spitting image. This artistic move by Hurston calls ahead to the second-wave feminist adage 'the personal is political' (and demonstrates through fiction the ways in which the political is also personal).[17]

Miscegenation, illegal at the time in the United States, is also brought to the fore in the novel. Anti-miscegenation laws in the United States were repealed only in 1967 with the Supreme Court case *Loving v. Virginia*. As Deniz Gevrek writes, such laws were primarily about 'regulating black/white interracial marriage', and the win forced sixteen Southern states to strike down the laws and rework their legal landscape when it came to interracial couples.[18]

How could the personal not be political when the rape of Black women by white men had been occurring for centuries? Beverly Guy-Sheftall and Johnnetta B. Cole write, 'under slavery, Black women's bodies were viewed as commodities, and used as a breeding ground for the reproduction of a slave population.' Moreover, 'enslaved Black women were also raped for the illicit pleasure of predatory white slave masters.' This continued violence perpetrated against Black women had manifold repercussions: 'lacking control of their sexuality and unable as mother[s] to protect their children from being sold, Black women have always occupied a precarious social space in American society.' Guy-Sheftall and Cole add: 'the deeply held belief that Black women are less valuable than women of other races/cultural groups – a legacy of slavery – pervades all aspects of American culture.'[19]

In *On Our Own Terms: Race, Class, and Gender in the Lives of African-American Women* (1997), Leith Mullings argues that depictions of African American women as sexually lascivious 'jezebel[s] functioned to excuse miscegenation' for white men and to excuse the sexual assault of Black women by white men.[20] It was not until the 1970s in the United States that a white male was successfully prosecuted for the rape of a Black woman. Hurston, writing in the 1930s, thus brings the nation's history as a slave nation to play in *Jonah's Gourd Vine*, as well as in her novels that followed. What results from such physical, psychological and emotional violence, the novel suggests, is a psycho-emotional distance and dissonance that can be seen in the main character and which ultimately leads to his death. In the novel, Hurston, the daughter and granddaughter of formerly enslaved people, exposes the unremitting direct and felt experiences of centuries of U.S. slavery on her characters, and in so doing reveals aspects of the Black experience for her contemporary audience.

The characters in *Jonah's Gourd Vine* are drawn close to home and surely show the influence of the years of field research that preceded Hurston's writing of the novel. Estranged from her father, John, at the time of his death, the novelist revisits her father's life, in particular his early and final years, in her first leading man. Hurston's father was also born into slavery. Like her father, John left his home community in search of freedom from his slavish, and formerly enslaved, stepfather. What John Pearson, perhaps similar to John Hurston, seems to crave most is the shelter and presence of a woman, one who does not ask questions of her husband and who has absolute faith in him. He finds such a person just before his death, his second wife, Sally, who provides John with both economic and emotional security in her devotion to and ostensible love of him.

John, then, seems to spend the entirety of his life seeking a return to the love and safety of his mother, Amy Crittenden. John is a man who as a boy was forced to leave behind a beloved mother and equally beloved siblings, having been pushed out of the home by the actions of his father, Ned. His family – like the family of his creator, Hurston – was taken from John, and its loss came at a time in his life when the dissolution could register and impact him profoundly. That is, his subsequent philandering in adulthood ties back to his relationship with his family, and in particular to his disrupted relationship with his enslaved Black mother, a relational dynamic that was in every way shaped and delimited by the system of legal slavery.

The implication, through the character of Ned, that colourism and intra-racism go two ways and are bound up with ideas of gender, as well as with ideas of biology and parentage, stands out. In this work, Hurston functions as both a novelist and a theorist on Black American culture, and by extension white culture. The Crittendens are poor sharecroppers in Alabama 'struggling to survive'. John and the other children 'work the land and help around the house', but, even with the children working to support the family, they remain stuck in poverty. The matriarch, Amy, adores her children, 'but she often finds herself at odds with Ned, who hates John . . . The sight of Amy's only biracial child irritates [him].'[21] When Ned looks at John, he sees the white rapist, and he turns the hate he has for John's biological father onto his son, beating and chastising him as if he were his slave master despite raising him and loving him from infancy. Ned's change in fondness for the boy comes about after being teased by his Black male friends for his love of, and doting behaviour towards, John as a baby – the suspicion being that this was because Ned secretly favoured John's light skin and curly hair. Ned changes course by John's early teenage years and begins to speak to and treat John violently. Ned believes he is entitled to belittle and overwork John because he is the Black patriarch and John, despite not being his biological son, is living in his home. As Coretta M. Pittman writes in her book *Literacy in a Long Blues Note* (2022), 'life with Ned becomes unbearable for

John.'[22] John's love for and devotion to his mother have prevented him from responding violently to Ned, but ultimately John leaves home following a furious interaction. Fed up, John warns Ned, stating, 'Ah done promised Gawd and a couple uh other men tuh stomp yo' guts out nex' time you raise yo' hand tuh me.'[23] When his stepfather binds John to a white man, a farmer who was a notorious overseer during slavery, essentially selling John off to be worked like a slave, John and Ned battle: 'When Ned whirled about with the doubled trace-chin in his right fist he found not a cowering bulk of a boy but a defiant man, feet spread wide, a large rock drawn back to hurl.' It is evident to everyone that John must leave the home. Amy's son will not be a slave, whether literally or figuratively through suffering. 'It came to John like a revelation,' the narrator says. 'Distance was escape.'[24]

Ned Crittenden can be seen as representative of formerly enslaved generations of of Black Americans (as can the character of Nanny in *Their Eyes Were Watching God,* discussed later, of whom Hurston writes with a similar tone). Ned (as well as Nanny) might also be read as a fictionalized version of Hurston's maternal grandmother, Sarah Potts, a formerly enslaved Black woman who detested Hurston's father in part because he was half white. Sarah, by extension, did not like the grandchild who was most like her son-in-law: Zora. Hurston describes her maternal grandmother in *Dust Tracks on a Road* as a woman who 'glared at me like open-faced hell'.[25] Sarah advised Zora's mother to beat her as a way of breaking the young girl – 'Stomp her guts out! Ruin her!'[26] – and to stop what she saw as Zora's brazen lies, which Hurston herself (and her mother) regarded rather as storytelling and fancy. Ned speaks to John with absolute disdain, referring to him as a 'house n—' in the vernacular of both the antebellum and, the novel suggests, postbellum period. Ned seems to spit bile when referring to John as a 'yaller n—' before threatening in a rage to 'stomp [his] guts out'.[27]

Ned's language is reflective of his experience as a formerly enslaved African American. Ned speaks to John as if he is John's overseer, not his parent. Through his language and actions, Ned shows that he feels he is better than John, for he has not been tainted by white blood. (Though Ned is also surely jealous and resentful of John's wealthy, white biological father.) John feels Ned's slight, as does John's mother, Amy. Ned's reign is far-reaching, extending over his wife, his family, his home and, ultimately, the novel. No longer a presence after the first chapter, the patriarch Ned's ideas about Black Americans ('N—s wuz made tuh work'), his consideration of his children ('Dese younguns aint uh bit better'n me. Let 'em come lak Ah did') and his treatment of his wife and family ('Ned looked about and seeing no plate fixed for him uncoiled the whip and standing tiptoe to give himself more force, brought the whip down across Amy's back') mark him as the antihero of the novel.[28] Meanwhile, Amy's love for John, similar to her love of her other children, seems also to be informed by her experiences as a woman and mother under slavery. Amy fights – battles – to protect her children.

Although whiteness and white American characters are peripheral to Hurston's fiction (with the exception of her final novel, which centres around white Southerners), Hurston implicates and exposes the very systems that give shape to and circumscribe Black life and Black art during the periods in which her works are set. John's story is set during the post-Reconstruction period and is in every way informed by the system of slavery that all but guaranteed his birth. John is Amy's oldest son and her only mixed-race child, and the sole child born of Amy's rape by her white master, Alf, who is now a high judge deemed 'big wood' (that is, powerful and influential). All but John seem aware of his paternity; it is perhaps for this reason, the novel suggests, that he suffers from a kind of unseeing that is connected to a lack of interiority (that is, until the novel's end). His father is a judge and a white man who looks exactly like him, and yet even in his presence, John cannot recognize this fact. Why would he? He was born during the antebellum period but came of age and consciousness after the abolition of slavery. As Pittman writes, 'John's paternity is never clarified [in the novel], but Alf seems to recognize something about the young man at their first meeting, telling John "your face looks sort of familiar but I can't place you".'[29]

Innumerable numbers of known biracial sons born to enslaved Black women and enslaving white men were walking around the South or working hard labour for their white biological fathers. Some were aware of their paternity and others perhaps not. John was not an anomaly with regard to the circumstances of his life and birth. Yet, perhaps John is anomalous in that only he cannot seem to see and thus know what is right in front of him. Pittman suggests that 'Alf shows affection toward John' in employment and other ways, and concludes that 'Alf's encouragement . . . may be because John is his son, and he wants the young man to at least have a functional level of literacy and to be a good person.'[30]

When John is away from home philandering, a habitual occurrence, Lucy gives birth to a child, a girl. With John away, Lucy is vulnerable to and accosted by her brother, Bud Potts (Potts being Hurston's maternal surname), who demands she pay him back the $3 that John borrowed from him. When Lucy tells her brother to come back when John is home so that her husband can pay him, Bud demands of Lucy, who at this time is in labour, 'Gimme mah money and lemme go "fo" Ah git mad.'[31] Bud 'looked around him contemptuously' before dismantling Lucy's bed, which was 'down in a twinkling, the feather mattress and bolster heaped upon the floor, while Bud dragged out the head and foot pieces'.[32] Lucy sinks 'down upon the mattress and [fights] the lump in her throat', before sending one of her son's to get help.[33] When John, who has been 'all 'round de jook behind de cotton gin wid Delphine' – that is, having an affair – returns home to find his wife and new baby on a 'pallet on the floor', he sees red.[34] John locates and beats Lucy's brother, 'and steals a pig to feed John's family', winding up imprisoned as a result.[35] There is to be a trial, but the white authorities have already decided that John will be beaten, and then be put on the chain-gang. John determines once again that he must flee, but he is rescued from his fate when Alf Pearson 'ask[s] that the prisoner be released in[to] his charge'.[36] The narrator provides that 'nobody touched John as he drove Judge Pearson home.'[37] Alf advises John when 'gifting' him $50 to escape Notasulga, Alabama (the very place from which Hurston's parents relocated around 1893),

Of course you did not know. Because God has given to all men the gift of blindness. That is to say that He cursed but few with vision. Ever hear tell of a happy prophet? This old world wouldn't roll on the way He started it if men could see. Ha! In fact I think God Himself was looking off when you went and got yourself born.[38]

John thinks Alf is talking about the events that led to his imprisonment. Rightly so, as Alf begins with, 'I'm not going to ask you why you've done these things, partly because I already know, and partly because I don't believe you do.'[39] What Alf Pearson knows exactly, he never says. He also never clarifies the meaning for John and instead 'laugh[s] sardonically' before launching into his ostensible theory of God, and of the circumstances of John's birth. 'God' was not in fact 'looking off' but rather imprinting John with his biological father's physical stature and features, including a seemingly curious and brazen personality and charm. Alf continues,

John, distance is the only cure for certain diseases. Here's fifty dollars. There are lot of other towns in the world besides Notasulga, and there's several hours before midnight . . . Good bye, John. I know how to read and write and I believe Lucy [John's wife] does too.[40]

Not only does Alf help John escape a judicial system stacked against him, but he reminds his biological son of the difference between his mother, Amy, and his wife, Lucy. Alf and Lucy can read as they are freeborn, whereas Amy cannot as she was born into slavery and denied by law the right to learn to read or write. Alf also suggests that he is available to John, and reachable by way of letter. Following this conversation, the narrator tells us that 'In the early black dark John was gone.'[41]

Alf Pearson is a judge; he is 'big wood' and not 'brush', and he is a white man; John was bound to listen to him.[42] It is by way of Alf's money, with which John purchases a train ticket, that John rides on 'a railway coach for the first time in his life, though he hid this fact from his traveling mate'. Significantly, the narrator tells us that for John, 'nothing in the world ever quite equaled that first ride on a train' (a moment of foreshadowing, as John is killed by a train at the novel's end).[43] His marriage to Lucy, the birth of his eight children, his later role as pastor of his church: none of these will equal his experience of that train ride. In this moment, the distraction of a spiritually lost man meets the technology of the railroad; and later, what was begun with wonder and the spirit of exploration will end in tragedy.

Hurston's novel begins during the era of Reconstruction in the United States. As with most Black families at that time – with Amy, a housewife, perhaps the one exception – all members of the family work outside the home as farmhands. They are a sharecropping family, and their present and future is thus bound up in a system that, according to Angela Davis, 'wanted to replicate the antebellum conditions' of life for African Americans in the South.[44]

John's mother, Amy, a fierce protector, was born into slavery and emancipated following the Civil War. Fought between 1861 and 1865, the Civil War ended 240 years of slavery in the USA. What this meant for the 4 million or more formerly enslaved Africans and African Americans was freedom, yes, but also dispossession. The 'crushing burden of white supremacy' not only circumscribed Black people's lives but 'limited their hopes and aspirations', especially after 'the U.S. government abandoned black people in the south to white southerners and their state and local governments'.[45] The federal government, which 'had affirmed [African Americans'] rights as citizens during Reconstruction', subsequently 'ignored the legal, political, and economic situation that entrapped most black southerners'.[46] Contemporaneous white America 'regarded black Americans as an inferior race not entitled to those rights that the Constitution supposedly guaranteed'.[47] It would be improbable, impossible, for some Black Americans not to also imbibe these deadly, dehumanizing approaches to their fellow Black citizens.

It is only upon his leaving his family that John Pearson gains his paternal name, provided to him by his mother as he departs. Similar to Hurston's own father, whose mother's story under slavery mirrors Amy's in this way, John Pearson is the very embodiment of rape, miscegenation and slavery; he is also a living, breathing manifestation of the racialized and gendered power of his white paternity, and the real and relative powerlessness of Black women within that same system. (During the time that miscegenation laws were enacted in the United States, while marriage was outlawed between Black Americans and white Americans, sex between these two groups, while taboo, clearly was not.) Both John and Amy are marked by slavery – and so, we can argue, is Alf. *Jonah's Gourd Vine* presents slavery as a still present physical, economic, emotional, familial, spiritual and psychic caul over a people and a nation.

It is perhaps not a surprise that John does not survive. His legacy, informed as it is by wilful blindness, by cruelty, greed, horror and the privileges that accrue to beneficiaries of a white supremacist nation, does not seem to allow for a triumphant ending. Why? His vision is limited. His sight and insight have been tampered with by others, by society, as well as by his limitations as a human subject born at a particular time, in a particular nation and to a particular woman and man. John seems to be running from himself, running from his first family, running from the community of white people who would hang him and the community of Black people who would see him re-enslaved as a sharecropper; he is also, through extramarital affairs, running from the banality and finality of Lucy and their children.

John departs the train in Sanford, Florida, where he finds work in a railroad camp. He sends money home to Lucy and the children, hears talk about a town called Eatonville, finds a job working for Sam Mosely, 'the second most prosperous man in Eatonville',[48] and, after a year and a bit of fun living on his own, John sends for Lucy and the children. Lucy castigates John for his absence, but upon her arrival to Eatonville she 'sniff[s] sweet air laden with nigh-blooming jasmine and wished that she had been born in this climate'.[49] In Eatonville, John gains popularity as an itinerant minister and soon after lands his own congregation, Zion Hope. The family stabilizes for a time, and John and Lucy's marriage produces seven more children, the last of whom is born shortly before Lucy's early demise. Although

Lucy's cause of death is not given, the suggestion of the novel is that Lucy dies from a broken heart. Her death quickly follows a marital argument in which Lucy accuses John of 'living dirty', and John gives Lucy a 'resounding smack'.[50] John quickly remarries to a younger woman named Hattie Tyson, who is given to drinking and partying and who is believed by the community to have put a hex on John – a hex that John and Lucy's community believe expedited Lucy's end and drew John to Hattie. John's marriage to Hattie quickly dissolves, but not before John's reputation is ruined among his friends and congregation. Following his divorce from Hattie, John relocates to Plant City, Florida, where he soon meets Sally Lovelace, who becomes John's third and last wife.

John walks alone in the world, seemingly unaware of or detached from his responsibility to his children. His concern always seems to be with his own well-being, or at the end, his new wife, Sally. John's insularity, his myopia and ultimately his seeming indifference to his children function as actual and metaphoric barriers to sight, vision and internal reflection. John has been all-action since leaving his mother's home, but in Plant City he meets Sally, 'a tall black woman who smiled at him over a gate. Yard chock full of roses in no set pattern.'[51] From her deep front porch, 'smothered in bucket flowers', the street and world look and seem 'so different' to John, as if 'changed in a dream way'.[52] Sally – her wealth and beautiful home, and her full acceptance of her husband – seems to foster a change in John, such that he for the first time ponders the reality of the world: '"Maybe nothin' ain't real sho 'nuff. Maybe 'tain't no world. No elements, no nothin'. Maybe wese jus' somewhere in God's mind," but when he wiggled his tired toes the world thudded and throbbed before him.'[53] Sally is prosperous, widowed and propertied. Like his mother, and like Lucy, Sally steps in to rescue John from the challenges of his life, but their love affair is truncated by John's untimely death. John's car is struck by a train on a return trip from Sandford, where he had gone to visit friends at Sally's prompting. Sally had purchased the car for John, and while he was in Sandford, he used it to drive around a woman named Ora, whom he also slept with 'in a dingy back room in Ovieda'.[54]

Hurston closes *Jonah's Gourd Vine* with the scene of John's funeral: 'So at last the preacher wiped his mouth in the final way and said, "He wuz uh man, and nobody knowed 'im but God," and it was ended in rhythm. With the drumming of the feet, and the mournful dance of the heads, in rhythm, it was ended.'[55] Alan Brown writes that with the character of John Pearson, a biracial subject existing within a segregated u.s. society heavily informed by a white supremacist, nationalist Christian ethos, Hurston 'unearthed a tragic element that no previous black writer had found in that most prestigious of black institutions, the preacher'.[56] As the daughter of a Black preacher herself, this was ripe creative material from which Hurston could draw. Brown reads *Jonah's Gourd Vine* as the story of 'one man's attempt to come to terms with the nature that dwells on the inside and on the outside of all of us', and therefore as 'more than just a regional or an ethnic novel'. Rather, in 'John Pearson's inability to resolve the conflict that exists between the physical and spiritual forces', the novel is suggestive also of 'society's and, ultimately, mankind's tragedy as well'.[57]

John Pearson is a character one both loves and abhors, both pities and admires. He is at once a man and a boy. John, who is a father of eight children, strays – in his marriages, in his mind and in his life. The suggestion of the novel is that John was 'big wood' not because of his white, slave-owning paternity, but because he is physically beautiful, charismatic, smart, questing and gifted, not to mention a philandering lover and neglectful father. The new era with its new technologies (in the guise of the train) is a foreign and ultimately inhospitable land for a man such as John Pearson.

Originally published in 1935 by Lippincott, Hurston's folklore collection *Mules and Men* was the first such to be written by an African American woman scholar. In *Folkore Concepts: Histories and Critiques* (2020), a collection of essays by folklorist Dan Ben-Amos edited by Henry Glassie and Elliott Oring, folklore is considered to be 'a culturally unique mode of communication [that] exists in any society'. It has a distinctiveness [that] is formal, thematic, and performative . . . There is a correlation between these three levels of expression, by which the speakers of folklore set it apart from any other communication in society . . . [Folklore] could be traditional, but it is not so by definition; it could be anonymous, but it is not essentially so . . . [A]ny of the qualities that were, and still are, attributed to folklore might be inherent in some forms, in some cultures, and anytime [*sic*] that they are, it is up to the folklorists to demonstrate it anew.[58]

Enter Hurston's *Mules and Men*, a collection of seventy tales, including work songs, children's games, legends, adult card games, dance and even party performances. Written in both standard English and AAVE, *Mules and Men* brings together close to six years of field research by Hurston in the southeastern United States, particularly Florida. In presenting her research and scholarship in the collection, Hurston writes not in the high formalism – and, in some ways, esotericism – of academic speak but rather in the relaxed, less formal (though still structured) speech of a conversation between people seeking some measure of mutual understanding. It is as if Hurston is saying to her audience of readers, *Have I got a story for you. Buckle up, and learn while you enjoy.*

The edifying elements of *Mules and Men* share space with Hurston's aesthetics as a novelist. Indeed, Hurston prepared *Mules and Men* as she simultaneously wrote her first novel. The influence and confluence of analytical and research-based writings with the imaginative cannot be missed with this work (especially if one listens to the superb audio recording of the book by the late actress and activist Ruby Dee). bell hooks argues that Hurston presents herself as 'just plain folks' in *Mules and Men*, thus enabling 'the uninformed non-academic reader to feel less distanced from the process of anthropological work'.[59] Thus hooks deems *Mules and Men* 'not fully accurate': Hurston 'wanted her collection of folklore to sell' and so 'distort[ed] the truth'.[60] Marjorie Pryse argues that 'many of the tales Hurston transcribes [in *Mules and Men*] show black people trying to explain the riddles of the universe – why

they are poor, why they are black, and where they came from.'[61]
Mules and Men 'gave [Hurston] the authority to tell stories because
in the act of writing down the old "lies," Hurston created a bridge
between the "primitive" authority of folk life and the literary power
of written texts.'[62] Robert Hemenway writes that Hurston's 'fiction
represented the process of folkloric transmission, emphasizing
the ways of thinking and speaking which grew from the folk
environment'.[63]

The writer Sophie Abramowitz gives context to the disciplinary
field that Hurston had entered and through which she was to
solidify her voice and perspective. She writes,

> the racist and racialist ideas of culture that influenced [the
> discipline of] folklore of the 1920s and 1930s, folklore in which
> Hurston would locate herself and work, and at the same time
> expand on the discipline, can be traced to the same sources as
> those that informed anthropology and its cultural turn during
> the era.[64]

Anthropology and eugenics, Abramowitz explains, 'were leveraged
together explicitly in order to develop immigration restrictions
and sterilization laws', and they were 'exported as structures
undergirding popular representations of Blackness through
minstrelsy and other performances'.[65] Abramowitz adds that 'both
pseudo-sciences provided a racial logic to the resurgence of the Ku
Klux Klan in the 1910s', and that 'adherents from both [fields of
study] were also involved in the formation of folklore as a practice
and a discipline.'[66] This was the cultural and disciplinary framework
with which Hurston contended both as a student and later as a
seasoned scholar. Her 'genre-bending folkloric work was both born
from and in reaction to this moment'.[67]

Franz Boas wrote the introduction to *Mules and Men,* and
in doing so positioned himself as intellectually supportive of
Hurston. Hurston's craft and skill as both a storyteller and a writer
are evident in the book. bell hooks writes, 'retrospectively, the
introduction to *Mules and Men* can be seen as testimony, bearing

witness to the "fictive" scholar/anthropologist Hurston created for the sake of her work and the sake of her narrative.'[68] Hurston, hooks says, omits certain truths: '[She] does not tell readers that her initial attempts to gather material failed because she approached folks as though her training set her apart, maybe even above them, and that as a consequence she changed that approach.'[69] Hurston initially worked to maintain objective distance between herself and her subjects, in accordance with her academic training, but this led to 'failure to accomplish all she hoped for'.[70] Taking time to critically re-evaluate her approach, Hurston henceforth worked 'to establish intimate ties with' her subjects and adopted a system of 'participant observation' that informed her anthropological work going forward.[71] Hurston kept most of her struggles, creative and otherwise, from the eyes of her reading audience. She would not have detailed her struggles as a professional in *Mules and Men* any more than she would have done in a private conversation, and Hurston was a very private woman, especially about her work.

Hurston's was a perspective informed by being born and raised in the South to parents with direct experience of legal bondage. Her perspective was also informed by her elite education at universities in the North, as well as by her attendance, while a student at Howard University, at salons held by the poet Georgia Douglas Johnson, which were also frequented by W.E.B. Du Bois, Alain Locke and other Black luminaries of the time. Hurston's approach to her Black subjects, who lived in the same town she had grown up in, ultimately became her approach to herself as a writer, thinker and artist.

In her work as an anthropologist and folklorist, Hurston collected and codified both contemporary and earlier folklore of Black Americans in the U.S. South, spanning the close of the nineteenth century to the 1930s. *Mules and Men* educated its readers – a white audience – about not only their nation's culture and history but the influence of Black arts and Black language on that culture. Put another way, in collecting, documenting, categorizing and writing up for a more general readership her three years of field notes into a cohesive narrative, Hurston was able to tell a story of a particular segment of Black America at a particular time in U.S.

history. The story Hurston wrote is a commingling of the fictive and the real, a blend that arose from the imagination of a gifted storyteller and practised researcher.

Mules and Men educates readers on Negro folklore – that is, the ideas, stories and histories of Black Americans passed through oral tradition – and what this nomenclature entails, encompassing a variety of forms including language, dialect, music, art and characteristic linguistic expressions. Hurston tells us at the opening of the book her reason for choosing the topography, if not the people, of her first fieldwork project: 'Florida is a place that draws people – white people from all over the world, and Negroes from every Southern state surely and some of the North and West.'[72] She continues, 'So I knew that it was possible for me to get a cross-section of the Negro South in the one state. And then I realized that I was new myself, so it looked sensible for me to choose familiar ground.'[73] Hurston is careful to underscore in her introduction to *Mules and Men* that her interest in returning home was not to flaunt her success or 'so that the home folks could make admiration over me because I had been up North to college and come back with a diploma and a Chevrolet'.[74] Indeed, she writes, 'I knew they were not going to pay either one of these items too much mind.'[75] Hurston thus shows, or performs, a professional humility in her book's introduction, even as she asserts her credentials and the fact that she owned a car at a time when few Americans, regardless of race, would have had the privilege.

Until the age of thirteen, Hurston had, as she writes it, a relatively normal childhood that included play, going to church and school, being chided by her parents, doing chores and so forth. This normality, and the nuclear family, fell away for Hurston and her siblings after 1904. It seems appropriate that feeling emotion – that is, the inability to remain purely objective – would inform the work of the researcher, whether knowingly or not. I think it is possible to see an element of nostalgia in Hurston's thoroughgoing valuation and celebration of these communities and the particular Black folks she captures. Hurston writes that she 'hurried back to Eatonville' as she considered it a relatively safe place for her to carry out her work, since it was once her home community: she 'knew that the town was full of material and that [she] could get it without hurt, harm or danger'.[76] She was compelled by memories of her childhood, such as when she was sent to Joe Clarke's store by her mother to secure an ingredient needed to complete a meal: little Zora would linger and listen to the men, and sometimes women, 'gather on the store porch of evenings and swap stories'.[77] There must, then, have been some nostalgia influencing Hurston's choice of Eatonville to collect folklore.

Hurston's research-subjects-become-characters, *Mules and Men* suggests, constitute the Southern Black labouring classes in their full cultural and regional diversity. Living in an almost entirely Black societal landscape, they are representative of Black folklore and Black folk culture, seen in everything from their speech patterns to their understanding of and engagement with both God and the Devil. These are not simple people, the book suggests: they have a language, or multiple languages; a culture; and a code of behaviour that is gendered and nuanced with regard to factors such as economics and skin tone. As the Hurston scholar Dana McKinnon Preu writes, the collection 'is unique not only because it preserves oral literature, but because as a literature writer, Hurston has created an authentic oral world/culture as the context for the literature'.[78] She continues, 'Because of Hurston's fusion of anthropological research and literary creation, *Mules and Men* is unique in preserving a vital recording of a functioning Afro-American oral culture.'[79]

As Beulah S. Hemmingway notes, in *Mules and Men*, 'Hurston's characters are . . . sophisticated people who conjure up the memory of an old black saying: "A heap sees, but few knows".' It would be unwise to 'mistak[e] the shallowness of our own understanding for the shallowness in the people we study'.[80] *Mules and Men* showcases Black Americans as complex, undiminished by white supremacy and by white cultural apartheid. That is, Hurston writes the people in the collection as multifaceted and human. She provides readers a glimpse into the reality of her research when she writes, 'Folklore is not as easy to collect as it sounds,' explaining that this is often because 'the best source is where there are the least influences and these people, being usually under-privileged, are the shyest. They are most reluctant at times to reveal that which the soul lives by.'[81]

Again, memory serves here as a framework for movement in *Mules and Men*: 'I thought about the tales I had heard as a child' – tales of 'how the devil always outsmarted God', or of figures like Brer Fox or Brer Rabbit, who 'were walking the earth like natural men way back in the days when God himself was on the ground and men could talk with him'.[82] Readers familiar with AAVE, and also perhaps readers familiar with the Appalachian dialect as well as a particular white Southern vernacular, will recognize some of the phrases Hurston uses to characterize her subjects. Those unfamiliar with Black English but who understand the phonetic dimensions of language need only read the tales and songs included in *Mules and Men* aloud and listen for context while reading.

In featuring her automobile, a used Chevrolet that she named 'Sassy Susie', and describing her drive down to Eatonville, she is surely marking herself as a contemporary, modernist and New Negro subject. Sassy Susie becomes a character in the book as well as a technological means by which Hurston can win over her subjects. The vehicle helps Hurston not only to travel around as she is collecting, but to draw attention to herself. It also allows for the creation of a character through which Hurston can situate herself as researcher-subject. For example, Hurston writes, 'I staggered sleepily forth to the little Chevrolet for Eatonville. The car was overflowing with passengers but I was so dull from lack of sleep that I didn't know who they were. All I knew is they belonged to Eatonville.'[83] Hurston represented one of the less than 20 per cent of Americans who owned a car in 1928. Hers was purchased second hand for $300. Her brother John had accompanied her to the dealership – the entrenched patriarchal and racialized gender politics of the time dictated less a need and more a requirement of his presence, ostensibly in place of Hurston's father.

As Mary Helen Washington writes, *Mules and Men* demonstrates that Hurston 'not only celebrated the distinctiveness of black culture, but saw those traditional black folkways as marked improvements over the "imaginative wasteland of white society"'.[84] She continues, '[*Mules and Men*] goes far beyond the mere reproduction of the tales'. The book 'introduces the reader to the whole world of jook joints, lying contests, and tall-tale sessions that make up the drama of the folk life of black people in the rural South'.[85] Through her narrative style – with the tales 'set in the framework of a story in which Hurston herself is a character' – the book becomes unlike 'conventional folklore collections [where subjects] are merely informants'. The people featured in *Mules and Men* 'are real personalities . . . exposing their prejudices, love affairs, jealousies, while they tell the old stories about how black people got black or how John outwitted Ole Massa during slavery'.[86]

Through the writing and revising of the collection – with editorial feedback from not only her editor at Lippincott but Mason and Locke – Hurston was also developing as a writer. She became practised at writing dialogue, at characterization, setting and tonality, and melding AAVE and Standard English in her fiction and non-fiction alike. Simultaneous to the writing of *Mules and Men*, Hurston was drafting what would become her third novel, *Moses, Man of the Mountain*, commonly read by literary critics as a retelling of the Book of Exodus from the Old Testament. More recently, however, critics have read the novel as a rejection by Hurston of both the myth and of Moses as a liberatory figure for African Americans. In my reading of *Moses*, I align with both groups but also regard the book as an allegorical expression of the life of its author. In this light, the book might be read as a final farewell to Hurston's African American subjects, and thus a goodbye to the limited and circumscribed African American subjectivity that Hurston was aiming to break free from. For *Moses* is, after all, the last novel in which Hurston directly took up the subject of the African American as a character. *Moses* might be read as an allegory of Hurston's life to date. She too was touched by the divine (in her own way), and she too could turn a staff into a divining rod or a serpent – but she did this by way of the pen and the typewriter.

As Hurston writes Moses, he is a man, a diviner and a patriarch. Like all patriarchs, and perhaps like all men, Moses is fallible, prone to violence and can prove punishing, cruel and unpredictable. Moses, too, is accustomed to being catered to, by turns coddled and obeyed. He is an ambivalent, though committed, ruler whose religious faith has been imprinted on him by another, older man, a magician who not only befriended Moses but in time became his father-in-law: Jethro. Moses has thus grown into a man of great power under the tutelage of an influential man with his own profound belief in a God of the Mountain.

Hurston writes towards the close of the novel, 'Moses took his rod and set out and the people saw him. And many feelings followed him as he went. Some thought ambitious thoughts and all of them thought awe.'[87] He is a respected, revered and by turns despised figure who engenders deep feeling in others. When Moses ascends Mt Nebo at the novel's end, he seats himself 'on the peak of Pisgah' and looks 'both ways in time'.[88] Looking down to see 'the tents of Israel spread out like the pattern of a giant rug', Moses thinks it 'A splendid and orderly sight – a magnificent spectacle,' lingering on it 'a long time with his eyes'.[89] Moses sees, takes in and loves the people he has led and with whom he has endured and overcome strife. He is also exhausted by the effort of leading the wilful and stubborn – 'good fighting men who would die for the glory of the tabernacle of Israel', as well as those who taxed his resolve, patience and commitment to his mission. The narrator continues, 'The sounds of Israel's existence came up to him. The lowering of herds, hammering of metal, sounds of strife, of crying and dying and sounds of song.' Significantly, the narrator adds, 'Moses felt happy over that.'[90] This is a despot looking not on people he despises, but on subjects who are besotted with him. This is a man and a leader taking in, for what he senses may be the last time, the wonder and vastness of what he sees when he looks high, as well as low. Moses sees value and humanity, and he feels happiness in that moment as a result.

Moses discovers hard-won lessons through his attempt to lead the Israelites out of bondage and to the Promised Land of his, and God's, vision. As he sits atop Pisgah, 'Nebo's highest peak', and looks down upon Israel, he realizes that 'no man may make another free,' as 'freedom [is] something internal'; rather, 'All you could do was give the opportunity for freedom and the man himself must make his own emancipation.'[91] We are told that 'No man on earth had ever wielded so much power' as Moses, who, despite his disinterest in ruling, 'had been thrust into the position of absolute rule- and law-giver'.[92] What human, what man, would not falter in possessing such authority? What man would not at times seem to be a despot, a zealot, even a lunatic? Moses, 'solitary figure on the peak', is a man 'fighting . . . all his wars, agonizing in wildernesses and deserts, facing revolts of Princes of Israel who had been slaves or the sons of slaves before he lifted his rod in Egypt' and wondering about the 'something [that] made him endure it all'.[93] Somewhat forlorn, and feeling as though 'he had failed in his highest dreams', Moses recognizes also that 'he had succeeded in others'. He determines that 'perhaps he had done as much as it was possible for one man to do for another', and that although Israel 'might not be absolutely free inside . . . he had taken from them the sorrow of serving without will, and had given them the strife of freedom'. The narrator continues, 'He had called to their memories the forgotten words of love and family . . . and the blessing of being responsible for their own.'[94] Moses is not bereft here, but he does believe it will take another generation, at least, for Israel to rid itself of an at first forced and then internalized slavishness. In the meantime, Moses thinks, 'Israel had her songs and singers. Israel had a fine army of fighters. Israel had laws on tables of stone and Israel had a God.'[95] Hurston's Moses is a reluctant and challenged leader who out of necessity and frustration – as well as growing knowledge of himself and mankind – unleashes his wrath on those whom he leads.

The book describes how 'out of a rotting mass of creeds', Moses 'had made a religion that had height and depth'.[96] Being human, 'he had made his mistakes and had his regrets.' These mistakes and regrets are present in his heart – as the narrator states, 'every heart has its graveyard.'[97] The awe that accompanies Moses as he walks away from Pisgah, towards his destiny – that is, Mt Sanai and beyond – is a result of both the man himself and the divine Christian God, made manifest through him: 'But some things had been well done. Now God had a voice and a glory.'[98]

The scholar Robert J. Morris considers *Moses* to be Hurston's 'most ambitious novel . . . [and] the most neglected of her four'.[99] He contends that there are three significant reasons for this neglect. First, the novel has suffered a lack of critical attention because in it Hurston does not centre a woman, proto-feminist or otherwise, as her protagonist, but rather a racially and ethnically ambiguous man. Second, owing to its biblical setting, *Moses* 'does not come within the bio-geographical frame that interests many Hurston scholars'.[100] Morris speculates further that another reason for the critical neglect of *Moses* might be that 'it is unclear what Hurston intended *Moses* to be and to mean.'[101] But *Moses, Man of the Mountain* is quite simply the story of a man, a myth and a people. It is a story that was first told and passed down orally and then codified in print, before again being passed down, and in turn refashioned, by word of mouth.

Hurston writes: 'The voice of the thunder leaped from peak to plain and Moses stood in the midst of it and said "Farewell." Then he turned with a firm tread and descended the other side of the mountain and headed back over the years.'[102] There is something tragic about this ending, in that Moses is alone and has 'turned away from his memories of fire-spitting mountains and night-vigils with God'.[103] This is a man exhausted by a mission he was disinclined towards but to which he committed himself for decades; he has given God all that he is going to give and thus returns a man to himself, by himself. Significantly, Moses does not martyr himself to a people, or to a God. Instead, he performs a return, 'back over the years', rendering possible the impossible; Moses belongs now to himself and is finally free – from his God, and from his and God's people.

The scholar Joshua Pederson writes that 'critics have never quite known what to do with *Moses, Man of the Mountain*,' citing a review by the twentieth-century African American novelist Ralph Ellison, who writes of the novel as having done 'nothing' whatsoever 'for Negro fiction'. White critics 'damned [the novel] with faint praise'; Pederson cites Percy Hutchison in the *New York Times*, who christened the book 'homespun' and as having an 'allure for the Negro's "primitive mind"'.[104] Hemenway dubbed the novel 'a noble failure' and, worse still, 'the victim of its own aspirations'.[105]

Pederson rightly argues that 'if *Moses* does not always feel of a piece, however, its fragmentation is less a flaw than a necessary part of the design.'[106] He adds that Hurston's 'ambivalence about Exodus makes it unlikely that [she] intended her novel as a seamless "fusion", another clean appropriation of the Moses myth'.[107] Rather, as he sees it, Hurston employs a style which presages that of the novelist Ishmael Reed in *Mumbo Jumbo* (1972), writing that *Moses* adopts what Reed would later call 'gumbo style', a 'technique [that] might be the constant in African American literature, that of making something whole from scraps'.[108] Pederson concludes that *Moses* 'is [a] pastiche' of Exodus.[109] Like Reed, Hurston 'scramble[s] the race and ethnicity of [Moses] . . . in order to undermine easy racial identification'. In *Moses*, Pederson further argues, Hurston 'accentuates the negative aspects of . . . the Israelites' to suggest 'that these are figures not worth emulation', and Hurston takes 'careful aim at God, decentering the figure whose regard defines the Hebrews as divinely chosen'.[110] For Pederson, Hurston 'signif[ies] on Exodus in order to distance African-American history from an Israelite history that can no longer serve as a positive model for blacks'.[111]

Houston A. Baker Jr, a scholar specializing in the Harlem Renaissance, argues that 'Hurston's Moses experiences the world in "emergency mode",' and that, as such, 'The hermeneutics of Hurston's novel are a projection of the dynamics of post-traumatic slave syndrome[, which] is not stasis; it is not a becalmed genre painting of the horrors of the consequences' of the enslavement of the Israelites.[112] What Pederson thus reads in the novel as 'gumbo style' and pastiche, Baker identifies as Hurston's 'governing' as a novelist, which may be seen in her observations.[113] Neither the novel in itself nor the story of Moses is tidy; rather, both are contradictory, vast and human, which is to say fallible. As Baker sees it, the novel is an artistic expression of a 'brilliantly enumerated' idea by Hurston in her essay 'Characteristics of Negro Expression', included in Nancy Cunard's *Negro Anthology*. Baker writes, referencing Hurston's 'Characteristics', that 'premier among such characteristics were angularity and asymmetry.'[114]

The leading Hurston scholar Cheryl A. Wall writes of *Moses, Man of the Mountain* as featuring 'satirical sallies' that are 'invariably good-natured and often very funny', and '*not* the serious statement about faith and freedom [Hurston] seems to have intended'.[115] It is a challenge unmeasurable to attempt something that has not been seen before or attempted in recent and known herstory. Equally challenging is the expansion of a mindset in the absence of a rubric, ideology or framework by which to measure oneself by, follow or even reject. Perhaps Hurston's reviewers, grounded as they are in U.S. and Black American culture, cannot rid themselves of their and our (white supremacist) culture's impulse towards, or even need for, a ruler (in the figure of a charismatic leader, as in Hurston's novel), and as a result a rule-governed, lockstep life: one in which the status quo is readily accepted, rather than questioned or rejected. *Moses* is an indictment. As Hurston demonstrates through her figure of Moses, liberation comes from within. No one, and especially not (white) man, can lead another to their own personal liberation and freedom. This is the final lesson for Moses the man and for Hurston's readers of *Moses, Man of the Mountain*.

5

Stormy Weather

When Hurston signed her contract with Lippincott, she did so on the understanding that the novel she told them she was currently writing would manifest. That novel, *Jonah's Gourd Vine*, was published in 1934 to good reviews. On the strength of *Jonah's Gourd Vine*, Hurston signed a three-book deal with Lippincott that would include the publication of *Mules and Men*, *Their Eyes Were Watching God* and *Tell My Horse*.

Hurston did not have an agent at the time of signing her first contract and received a $200 advance for *Jonah's Gourd Vine*. Had she been a better supported or more materially stable writer, or a man, she would almost certainly have garnered a larger advance. When writing *Their Eyes Were Watching God*, Hurston stayed with what she knew. As with her first novel, this second one would also borrow, however loosely, from Hurston's personal life.

This second novel, published three years after *Jonah's Gourd Vine* and two years after *Mules and Men*, 'plots the long and torturous life' of Janie Crawford 'through several relationships and misfortunes, including the most calamitous natural disaster in modern Florida history, the drowning of more than two thousand persons on the south shore of Lake Okeechobee during the devastating 1928 hurricane'.[1] Henry Louis Gates Jr writes in the 'Afterword' to the 1998 edition of *Their Eyes Were Watching God* that the book is 'a lyrical novel [that] correlates the need of [Janie's] first two husbands for ownership of progressively larger physical space (and the gaudy accoutrements of upward mobility) with the suppression of self-awareness in their wife'.[2] Gates notes that because the novel charts

'Janie's journey from object to subject', this in effect renders the book 'a bold feminist novel, [and the] first to be explicitly so in the Afro-American tradition'.[3] Gates continues, 'in its concern with the project of finding a voice, with language as an instrument of injury and salvation, of selfhood and empowerment, *Their Eyes Were Watching God* suggests many of the themes that inspirit Hurston's oeuvre as a whole.' He adds further that Hurston's 'use of vernacular became the fundamental framework for all but one of her novels'.[4] Hurston uses free indirect speech in the novel as a way of 'signifying [Janie's] awareness of self' such that 'the narrative . . . shifts from third [person] to a blend of first and third person'.[5] The novel, then, according to Gates, charts the 'fulfillment of an autonomous imagination', that of the novel's protagonist, the mixed-race (Black and white) subject Janie Crawford.[6]

In my reading of Hurston's second and most famous novel, I build on the feminist philosopher and cultural theorist Susan Bordo's idea of materiality, and in particular her assertion that '"materiality", in the broadest terms, signifies . . . our finitude. It refers to our inescapable physical locatedness in time and space, in history and culture, both of which not only shape us . . . but also limit us.'[7] Bordo continues, 'As a cultural critic and a philosopher of the body, I explore and urge that we not lose sight of the concrete consequences – for "our bodies, ourselves" – of living in a gendered and racially ordered world.'[8] In Hurston's novel, the Black woman's body – Janie – can be read as a psycho-emotional and physical site, both directly and indirectly, such as through her generational DNA coding, agency and powerlessness.

The novel's protagonist, Janie Crawford, is fifteen at the opening of the novel. *Their Eyes Were Watching God* is set in the 1930s, in Florida, and spans the close of the nineteenth century and the first thirty years of the twentieth century. Mae G. Henderson writes that Hurston's second novel is a 'classic black woman's text [that] charts the female protagonist's development from voicelessness to voice, from silence to tongues'.[9] In this story within a story, Janie returns home to Eatonville, Florida, in her late forties with a tale on her tongue. The novel in fast order details Janie's life from her birth to the contemporary moment in which she relays to her good friend, Pheoby, her story. Janie is fifteen years old at the opening of the novel. Her mother, Leafy, who at seventeen was raped by her white male schoolteacher and impregnated with Janie, became an alcoholic, and soon after abandoned her infant to her mother, referred to as Nanny. Leafy has not been seen from since, and Janie is for all intents and purposes her maternal grandmother's daughter. Janie comes to consciousness, through her body and senses, at the novel's opening, and with limited to no awareness of the strictures of the Jim Crow world within and beyond her Nanny's gate. Janie is throughout the novel a body in motion – a modernist subject in the making and on the move. Both her development and her movements are shaped by the postbellum U.S. society in which she was born and is living in. Rather than the white supremacist (and Black heterosexist), heteronormative capitalist society designed to forestall the citizenship, rights, liberties and economic and cultural development of African American peoples, and Black women in particular, it is Nanny whom Janie sees as perhaps her greatest hindrance and enemy.

This animosity is in part because Janie does not know until her fifteenth year her grandmother's story. Nanny is called such because she was rendered a mammy under slavery and made to care for the white children of her mistress and master. Nanny was also raped by her master, by whom she conceived Leafy. Nanny tells Janie, 'You know, honey, us colored folks is branches without roots and that makes things come round in queer ways . . . Ah was born back in slavery so it wasn't for me to fulfil my dreams of whut a woman oughta be and to do.'[10]

Valerie Boyd suggests that *Their Eyes Were Watching God* 'is the story of . . . a deep-thinking, deep-feeling black woman who embarks on a quest for her own self'.[11] She writes of Nanny as an ex-slave 'who hopes to fulfil through Janie her own broken dreams'.[12] Janie grows up with white children, whom Nanny is hired by a white family to raise, so much so that she does not know or notice her racial and cultural difference from them. As Boyd posits, Janie 'doesn't even know she is black until she sees a picture of herself, when she is about six years old'.[13] Boyd reads the moment as showcasing Janie's lack of self-awareness: 'Hurston does not portray Janie's discovery as devastating.'[14] Janie, like her creator, is representative of both a New Woman and the making of a late 1930s New Negro subjectivity. Here is a New Woman and a New Negro combined, a Black woman character born and raised in the South who is the physical embodiment of the rapes of her mother and grandmother, and therefore of the white male authority and father. Janie is also, then, a new subject in American literature: although she is of mixed Black and white ancestry, she is not 'tragic' in the sense of the figure of the 'tragic mulatto' who does not fit into either world. In fact, by the close of *Their Eyes Were Watching God*, Janie is as near to triumphant as a Black woman of her time, situation and standing can be, even despite the devastating loss of her future husband, the beloved Vergible 'Tea Cake' Woods, the last and youngest of Janie's three husbands, who in order to save her own life Janie must kill. Janie is in mourning, but she is also free; through Tea Cake, she has known love that is committed, sensual and enlightening, and that is ultimately for Janie an avenue to greater awareness of herself, her community and the world in which she lives. Janie is once again in bloom at the close of *Eyes*, just as she was when a fifteen-year-old girl at the novel's opening.

In the second chapter of the novel, an important passage presents Janie's 'blossoming' in her youth:

It was a spring afternoon in West Florida. Janie had spent most of the day under a blossoming pear tree in the backyard. She had been spending every minute that she could steal from her chores under that tree for the last three days. That was to say ever since the first tiny bloom had opened. It had called her to come and gaze at the mystery. From barren brown stems to glistening leaf-buds; from the leaf-buds to snowy virginity of bloom. It stirred her tremendously . . . stretched on her back beneath the pear tree soaking in the alto chant of the visiting bees, the gold of the sun and the panting breath of the breeze when the inaudible voice of it all came to her. She saw a dust-bearing bee sink into the sanctum of the bloom; the thousand sister-calyxes arch to meet the love embrace and the ecstatic shiver of the tree from root to tiniest branch creaming in every blossom and frothing with delight. So this was marriage! She had been summoned to behold a revelation.[15]

By the close of the novel, Janie has been disabused of the idea of marriage by her first two marriages: her first husband she fled, and in the second marriage she was widowed. It is in her marriage to Tea Cake that Janie recovers her early conception of marriage as ecstatic and delightful. Janie becomes a physical manifestation of the promise and blossom of the pear tree of her youth, pollinated by nectar-seeking bees.

Their Eyes Were Watching God might be read doubly as a *Bildungsroman* and a *Künstlerroman*, a novel about the growth and development of an artist: in the book, Janie narrates her own story, in so doing demonstrating her artistry. Out of fear, Nanny marries Janie off to a much older Black man, Logan Killicks, who simply wants to use Janie as a mule. It takes twenty years and three marriages, the last of which is to the much younger Tea Cake, the love of her life, for Janie to transform back into the self-possessed and enterprising person she was at the novel's open. Before this can happen, however, Janie finds that she must kill, in self-defence, her beloved Tea Cake, who has been bitten by a rabid dog while trying to save Janie from drowning in the midst of a hurricane. Out of his mind with rabies, Tea Cake attempts to shoot Janie but misses, twice. Janie notices 'that even in his delirium he took good aim'.[16] Janie senses that 'the fiend in him must kill and Janie was the only thing living he saw.'[17]

By the end of the novel, Janie is a woman toting her own story. By killing off her young lover, Janie is liberated from marriage and from Black sexual politics altogether – that is, from men who claim ownership of her. Hurston, significantly, liberates Janie so that she belongs only to herself.

Hurston's *Their Eyes Were Watching God*, which centres a love story and features a Black heroine, was considered retrograde during a period in African American literature when protest literature was favoured. The sociologist Patricia Hill Collins notes that 'the transformed consciousness experienced by Janie, the light-skinned heroine of . . . *Their Eyes Were Watching God*, from obedient granddaughter to wife to a self-defined African American woman, can be directly traced to her experiences with each of her three husbands.' Collins continues, 'In one scene Janie's second husband [Joe 'Jody' Starks], angry because she served him a dinner of scorched rice, underdone fish, and soggy bread, hit her,' and this moment of physical violence 'stimulates Janie to stand "where he left her for unmeasured time" and think'. This 'thinking leads to the recognition that [Janie's] image of Jody tumbled down and shattered', and it is in this moment that Janie understands that 'she had an inside and an outside now and suddenly she knew how not to mix them.'[18]

Love is a centring force and theme in Hurston's signature novel. Ostensibly, romantic love drives the novel's plot repeatedly, but the protagonist's consciousness of *not* loving her grandmother, for example, also serves as a driving and divining force in the novel. Janie comes to knowledge of herself and the world like most people: in the context of her familial, romantic and marital relationships, as well as in the context of her relationship to the communities in which she finds herself, in this case both Black and white. Ultimately, the love affair at the centre of the novel is a conduit for the idea that love can be a vehicle to new life and new possibilities as well as a liberating force both in one's own life and in the world. By extension, love can also be and do the very opposite.

With *Their Eyes Were Watching God*, argues the scholar and activist Miriam DeCosta-Willis, Hurston combines 'the romantic plot and the quest plot', a common 'dilemma . . . in women's lives'.[19] Hurston engages this dilemma to carry Janie towards freedom and self-possession. The caveat is that Tea Cake must die a physical death to cement Janie as the 'hero of her own story' who 'searches for [and finds] autonomy and self-fulfillment'.[20]

DeCosta-Willis identifies 'tentativeness and self-doubt' as features that echo throughout literature written by women –

so too does a sense of the woman character as 'being in a state of suspension, of "moratorium"', which, she writes, 'Hurston's Janie' showcases.[21] Identifying more directly some of the factors playing into such characterization, the late theorist, civil rights activist and lawyer Pauli Murray wrote,

> When we compare the position of the black woman to that of the white woman we find that [the Black woman] remains single more often, bears more children, is in the labor market longer and in greater proportion, has less education, earns less, is widowed earlier, and carries a relatively heavier economic responsibility as family head than her white counterpart.[22]

Murray continues, 'a significant factor in the low economic and social status of black women is their concentration at the bottom rung of the employment ladder.'[23] She writes that Black women are daily 'confronted with the multiple barriers of poverty, race, and sex'.[24] Janie has no siblings and does not know her father. Her Nanny explains to her that her mother has run off but that she is still alive. By the time of Nanny's death, not long after Janie is married off to Killicks, Janie has become as her grandmother feared: a beautiful mixed-race young woman alone in the world. Nanny's worrying and working could not change that outcome. At the close of the novel, Janie is still a woman alone in the world, but by this time, Janie has the ability to see and control what is in her grasp, and in her midst. She has the home and the money necessary to do so – and, significantly, she has a friend in Pheoby.

The feminist author Tillie Olsen writes in *Silences* (1978) that writers need readers. As Hurston demonstrates in *Their Eyes Were Watching God*, storytellers equally have the need for listeners. Pheoby Watson, Janie's friend of twenty years, is the audience for and medium by which Hurston is able to employ the technique of the frame narrative – where an introductory narrative leads to the telling of another story – to tell Janie's story. Pheoby transforms after hearing Janie's story – as she says to Janie, she feels as if she 'done grown ten feet higher'.[25] When Janie has wrapped up her story, Pheoby adds, 'I ain't satisfied with myself no more' and tells of her plans to make her husband take her fishing. Before she leaves, Pheoby makes sure to let Janie know of her fidelity to her as a friend: 'nobody better not criticize you in my hearing.'[26] Janie responds with understanding, telling Pheoby, 'theyse parsed up from not knowing things,' and then offers up one of the most famous lines of the novel: 'It's a known fact, Pheoby, you got to go there to know there.'[27] The silence that follows Janie's statement allows for the two friends' independent thoughts, one of her living husband and hearth, and the other of her newly deceased husband and the times spent in their shared bedroom.

At the novel's close, Janie has returned to the house that Joe Starks bought and where for a time she made a home. She airs the house out and combs the 'road dust out of her hair'.[28] There then comes a 'sobbing sigh' as she thinks, 'singing and sobbing', about her lost love, Tea Cake.[29] This sighing, singing and sobbing does not last for long, as suddenly 'Tea Cake came prancing around her and the song of the sigh flew out of the window and lit in the top of the pine trees.'[30] Tea Cake's spirit has returned to Janie, and 'with the sun for a shawl', she speaks to her dead lover.[31] Janie calls out to her husband, at first unsure. Then she realizes, 'Of course he wasn't dead.'[32] The novel suggests that Janie and Tea Cake's love is infinite, not bound by the natural world. As the narrator states, 'The kiss of his memory made pictures of love and light against the wall . . . here was peace.'[33] Knowing peace, finally, Janie 'called in her soul to come and see'.[34]

In a way similar to *Jonah's Gourd Vine*, memory and song together close out the story of Janie Crawford in *Their Eyes Were Watching God*. Unlike in the former novel, the protagonist of Hurston's second novel, this time a Black woman, survives and lives to tell her story. While Tea Cake through his death engenders the telling of Janie's story and Pheoby serves as its necessary audience, Janie serves as the culture bearer, a rather conventional role for Black women specifically, and women generally. However, crucially here, the culture that Janie bears – that is, the story she carries, manifests and tells – is her own. With the novel, Hurston also enacts

A youthful and demure Zora. She looks concerned about something as she stands amid palm leaves, watching the sky or, as she might write it, 'God'.

a centring of an African American woman's life and story at a time of repression for Black women, making the novel revolutionary as well as, I suggest, emblematic of the protest literature of the era, of which Hurston was not but should have been regarded as a forerunner.

While writing *Their Eyes Were Watching God*, Hurston was also collecting for and writing a draft of her second folklore collection, *Tell My Horse*, a work published just one year following the publication of *Their Eyes*. In 1936 and 1937, Hurston received two Guggenheim Fellowships, which she used to underwrite fieldwork in Jamaica and in Haiti. This was the 'foreign' component of Hurston's fieldwork as an anthropologist and folklorist. The 1936 trip took Hurston beyond the U.S. Southeast and the Bahamas into the interior of Jamaica – in particular the Maroon community of Accompong, made up of descendants of African people who had escaped their enslavers – and Haiti, in particular on Gonâve Island. The visits occurred exactly ten years after Hurston was first in the field. Gone was the novice of yore, and in her place was a seasoned anthropologist, thinker and writer, a Black woman recognized for her work both as a novelist and, however begrudgingly for some, as a well-trained and practised researcher whose work had been published in seminal academic journals.

Tell My Horse, published in 1938, has both its champions and its disparagers, having been variously panned and praised across the decades. Many words have been written on Hurston's second and final published folklore collection, just as there continue to be many words written on its author. At the time, the book 'did not sell well' and its reception did not 'overwhelm'.[35] Hemenway considers it to be 'Hurston's poorest book, chiefly because of its form'.[36] Alain Locke claimed it was, simply, 'anthropological gossip'.[37] Hurston 'was a novelist and folklorist, not a political analyst or traveloguist', and *Tell My Horse* 'is filled with political analysis, often of a naïve sort, with superficial descriptions of West Indian curiosities'.[38] According to Hemenway, the work fails notably because it 'reports a good deal of public gossip as accepted fact'. Hurston, moreover, 'reveals a chauvinism that must have infuriated her Haitian hosts', as she 'consistently praises the nineteen-year occupation of that country by American marines, attributing solvency and political stability to the American influence'.[39] It is apparent that 'although she should have known better', as Hemenway writes, Hurston 'generalizes often' in the book. She 'gives a highly poetic account of Haitian history by describing its legendary status in oral tradition [but] makes no attempt to compare these legends to historical fact'.[40]

What Hemenway values about *Tell My Horse* is that (as in *Mules and Men*) Hurston's 'voodoo reporting . . . consistently treats voodoo as a legitimate, sophisticated religion' and, moreover, engages with the concept of zombies, 'supposedly soulless bodies called back from the dead'.[41] These soulless beings are not simply corpses risen from graves, but could be a person, 'of culture and refinement [who has] become a mindless beast of burden, toiling naked in a banana field, without any hope of release'.[42] While many would consider such creatures mere superstitious creations, Hurston had doubts.[43]

Hurston's original title for *Tell My Horse* was 'Bush', but during her first trip to Haiti, the final title came to her.[44] Valerie Boyd writes that the phrase, which in Creole is *Parlay cheval ou*, was one Hurston heard daily in Haiti: 'These were the words that the powerful and boisterous god Guede (pronounced geeday) said when he began to speak – always bluntly and always through a person he'd "mounted".'[45] The god Guede was 'never visible; this *loa* manifested himself by mounting someone, as a rider mounts a horse, then speaking and acting through his mount'. Boyd continues, 'A spirit "with social consciousness, plus a touch of the burlesque and slapstick", as Hurston described him, Guede always began his caustic commentary with these words, "Tell My Horse".'[46] By using *Tell My Horse* as the title of her second folklore collection, Hurston 'signaled her intent to speak bluntly in her book, to reveal things about Haiti and Jamaica that required courage to say'.[47] Whether Hurston did so is subject to debate.[48] She candidly offered a 'critique [of] the chauvinism . . . particularly in Jamaica' and her focus on voodoo shows 'great respect, reminiscent of [Hurston's] treatment of hoodoo in *Mules and Men*'.[49] In the words of Barbara Speisman, Hurston 'was no newcomer to the belief that voodoo was definitely a religion and an inherent part of Afro-American folklore' and that the 'Hoodoo doctors of the American South practice a religion every bit as strict and formal as that of the Catholic church'.[50] Speisman acknowledges the Hurston scholar Wade Davis, who, in his book *The Serpent and the Rainbow* (1987), 'gives . . . Hurston credit for being an extraordinary anthropologist who understood the logic of the voodoo culture not only in Haiti but in her American South'.[51]

Hurston was 45 years old when she made her way first to Jamaica and then to Haiti in 1936. In her subsequent visit to Haiti, in 1937, she had a greater desire to capture and put down for posterity the folklore of the peasant classes in both countries. Tellingly, Hurston located herself once again within all-Black communities in Jamaica, and in the Black republic of Haiti, to conduct her field research. For Hurston the source was always Africa and not Europe. Hurston saw, sensed and established in *Tell My Horse* a direct link between the Black communities of Jamaica, and in particular its Maroon villages, and the Republic of Haiti and West Africa. *Tell My Horse*, says Annette Trefzer, marked Hurston's 'leap beyond national boundaries' and is indicative of her 'cross-cultural interest in identity politics'.[52] Hurston was interested in fostering a 'trans-national understanding of African/American culture' and 'understood that voodoo served to marginalize Caribbean and African American cultures; therefore, she countered such political discourses with her discoveries about the global presence of spirit possession'.[53] Hurston's intellectual and imaginative trajectory in *Tell My Horse* is one of a reversal of the Middle Passage, the arduous leg of the triangular Atlantic trade route involving the journey from West Africa to the Americas. Hurston establishes an ontology – and thus a spiritual and cultural rootedness – for her Jamaican and Haitian subjects that is situated not in the West but rather in the African continent, specifically its westernmost region. These are West African-descended Western subjects of now Caribbean identity under study by a West African-descended Western subject of u.s. identity. As Hurston more than suggests, there are great and unaccounted-for similarities that link diasporic Black peoples, both culturally and in other ways. Simultaneously, there are chasms of difference that render any blanket assessment of Caribbean, American or diasporic Blackness both harmful and meaningless.

Tell My Horse reminds us that there are limitations to knowing, as well as limitations to access and knowledge. What the book ultimately provides is the situated standpoint of an anthropologist and writer at work, gathering 'like a broom' – as Hurston writes of herself in *Mules and Men* – the folklore of a people. *Tell My Horse*, however, undoubtedly bears the stamp and biases of Hurston, who from an anthropological perspective examines complex, diverse cultures that are not her own, and yet with which she shares cultural, spiritual and to an extent linguistic roots.

The phrase 'Tell my horse' suggests a belief in a spirit world, one linked to, yet beyond, the confines of Christianity, and rooted in Haitian Vodou. *Tell My Horse* is effectively a mount – the spirit of the author is upon the book and speaking through the book. Hurston the writer can say things that Hurston the woman cannot, and *Tell My Horse* is the means of enabling that voice to speak. Namely, Hurston highlights and challenges inter-ethnic intra-racism and colourism, as well as chauvinism, extant in contemporaneous Jamaican and Haitian society, while she simultaneously writes with wonder about these very societies. 'The very best place to be in all the world is St. Mary's parish, Jamaica,' wrote Hurston, despite writing in detail about the sex and gender chauvinism evident in the society she was studying.[54]

6

Featherbed Resistance

In spring 1941, Hurston relocated from New York to 1932 Hull Lane in Altadena, California, near Pasadena, in order to write her autobiography, which would be titled *Dust Tracks on a Road*. Katharane Edson Mershon, 'a wealthy friend', who according to Valerie Boyd was also an anthropologist, invited Hurston to move to her home.[1] Although reluctant to write an autobiography, Hurston settled in. Boyd writes that Mershon, 'a former dancer and instructor at Ruth St. Denis's famous Denishawn school . . . had conducted a clinic in Bali for years along with her husband, Jack.'[2] Recently relocated back to the United States, and 'anxious for intellectual stimulation . . . Mershon invited Hurston to be her houseguest for as many months as it might take her to finish her book.'[3]

Mershon was a good host who, according to Hurston, 'fed me well . . . called in the doctors and cleared the malaria out of my marrow, took me to I. Magnin's and dressed me up'.[4] In California, Hurston finished her first draft and, in addition to writing, toured the state with Mershon as her guide: 'I saw, and I saw and I *saw*!'[5] She visited 'the Pacific' and the

> Redwood forests, Golden Gates, cable cars, missions, gaps, gullies, San Simeon-with-William Randolph Hearst, Mon-Sur and Santa Barbara, Bay Bridges, and Giant Sequoia, Alcatraz, wharves, Capitol buildings, mountains that didn't have sense enough to know it was summer and take off their winter clothes, seals, sealrocks, and then seals on seal-rocks, pelicans and pelican rocks.[6]

Hurston seems to have been mesmerized by the Pacific Ocean. At first, Hurston drove herself and Mershon about, but eventually Mershon's husband chauffeured the two women. The two friends 'galloped from one end of the state [of California] to the other and from edge to ocean and back again' during Hurston's time off from writing. Hurston concluded 'this California is a swell state, especially from Santa Barbara on north' – which is where the money was – and that 'on the whole, California will do for a lovely state until God can make up something better.'[7]

Simultaneously – and presumably to make a living as well as with the hope of selling a script to one of the Hollywood studios – Hurston worked for Paramount Pictures as a story consultant from October 1941 to early January 1942. As Carla Kaplan writes, Hurston's 'interest in Hollywood had been building from the mid-thirties on, when she began regularly submitting her work to the studios.'[8] The novelist William Faulkner, like other white (male) writers of the period, had made good money screenwriting for Hollywood studios. Although studios did express interest in Hurston's writing, according to Kaplan – and in particular in *Jonah's Gourd Vine* – Hurston was never able to sell her work or have the kind of success that Faulkner was able to attain in Hollywood. Still, writes Kaplan, Hurston's 'work for film . . . *was* taken seriously by the studios'.[9] For example, *Their Eyes Were Watching God* 'was reviewed by Warner Bros. two months before its publication' and 'multiple studios reviewed *Dust Tracks on a Road* immediately upon publication'.[10] Hurston's fourth novel, *Seraph on the Suwanee*, for which Hurston received a $300 advance, 'was reviewed in galleys by both MGM and Warner Bros., and the latter considered producing a film'.[11]

By this time, Hurston was fifty years old, a celebrated writer and thinker, revered by some and rejected by others, and the most published Black woman writer of the first half of the twentieth century. Hurston had grown up in a community that understood the dangers of speaking too much and too freely. This was one of the reasons that Hurston's father and maternal grandmother were forever chastising and attempting to chasten Hurston as a young girl. Sharing too much with others could be dangerous, even deadly, for both the individual and her family and community. Hurston would have been taught to be tight-lipped about her life and circumstances even to those she most trusted, and even then to share only what she deemed necessary. Any idea that she would showcase the intimacies and intricacies of her life to a public reading audience would have been absurd to Hurston and perhaps even regarded as an insult. Kathleen Hassall writes that in *Dust Tracks on a Road*, Hurston 'conceals her date of birth . . . and expunges at least one husband'.[12] She continues, 'Some evidence suggests that Hurston silently edited ten years from her account.'[13] Hassall adds that the autobiography 'seems to spend a disproportionate number of pages on Hurston's earliest experiences in Florida, while leaving much of [Hurston's] adult life in shadow'.[14] *Dust Tracks on a Road* 'has little – eight pages altogether – to say about Hurston's career as the author of stories, plays, essays, three novels, and two books of folklore; it has almost nothing to say about her high-energy, high-impact part in the Harlem Renaissance'.[15] Hassall determines that 'Zora Neale Hurston was essentially a performance artist.'[16] She continues, 'As a black woman artist [Hurston] faced a daunting range of threats: opposition, silence [and] the deforming of her personality and her work. The performances helped her slip through the ropes.'[17]

Hurston completed the manuscript on 20 July 1941, and in 1942 Hurston was back on the East Coast, living in St Augustine, Florida, where she went to work revising it. Florida, living by the water, was where Hurston was always best able to write. In addition to finishing the draft of her autobiography, she spent 'the summer collecting folklore'.[18] She also lectured 'at Black colleges throughout the South' and published stories, editorials and reviews in publications such as *American Mercury* and the *Saturday Evening Post*.[19] That same year, Hurston was featured in *Who's Who in America*, *Current Biography* and *Twentieth Century Authors*.[20] In the last publication, she listed among her favourite authors Mark Twain, Charles Dickens, Sinclair Lewis and Anatole France.[21]

Written at the behest of Hurston's then publisher, Lippincott, *Dust Tracks on a Road*, published as it was in 1943, is notably an incomplete work, despite its high sales. As Hemenway, Boyd, Wall and other Hurston scholars have noted, the 1943 version of the book, published just after the Japanese attack on Pearl Harbor, was a sanitized edition in which Hurston's criticism of the USA as a nation of racial apartheid was excised. Nevertheless, it is also a remarkable and entertaining read. *Dust Tracks on a Road* as an invaluable work of self-fashioning and self-promotion, both of which Hurston must have felt were necessary to ensure the publication of her book and to draw in a readership. We might think of the book as her version of a creation myth. It is too easy to judge the actions of previous generations, especially when we know at first hand the challenges that accrue from daily living, let alone those that accrue for a Black woman artist as independent, self-respecting and reticent as Hurston was.

Written by a Black, feminist poet, writer and scholar, *Dust Tracks on a Road* should be celebrated for its mere existence and for the artistry contained within its pages – and for Hurston's unwillingness to tell readers any more about herself than she deemed acceptable, necessary or prudent. She was always a private person, one who focused on her art. Besides, and as most writers will affirm, writers tend to lie, or tell the truth slant, to paraphrase Emily Dickinson.[22] Hurston herself writes in *Dust Tracks on a Road* that 'anybody whose mouth is cut cross-ways is given to lying, unconsciously as well as knowingly.'[23] Narrative, Toni Morrison advised in her 1993 speech on winning the Nobel Prize in Literature, is in fact 'radical, creating us at the very moment it is being created'.[24]

The year after her autobiography was published, Hurston relocated from St Augustine to Daytona Beach, where she purchased the first of two houseboats, christening it *Wanago*. *Wanago* was 'a 32-foot [10 m] houseboat with 44 horsepower engine'.[25] She would live on houseboats for four years. Boyd writes that Hurston sailed *Wanago* on a 'solitary 1,500-mile (2,400 km) sea voyage [to] New York' in October 1944, in order to meet with publishers and to promote her autobiography. On Hurston's return to Florida, she 'replaced the weathered *Wanago* with a new boat, the *Sun Tan*'.[26] The same year, Hurston was also awarded the Anisfield-Wolf Book

Award for her autobiography. It was deemed 'the best book on race relations' and 'was featured on the cover of *Saturday Review*', which sponsored the award.[27] The award, established in 1935, came with a $1,000 prize. *Dust Tracks on the Road* continued to sell well.

By its very title, the work suggests a movement that is both physical and spiritual in nature, the 'dust' calling to mind not only the unpaved roads of the early twentieth-century rural South but the biblical language of Christian prayer: ashes to ashes, dust to dust. As well as tracks left by walking or by car tyres, 'dust tracks on a road' connotes dirt and, to some degree, toil. The title, then, is also a metaphor for class and caste – for 'people who walk in the dust', as Hurston writes in the book.[28] She clearly counted herself as being among those who walk in the dust.

Hurston's ideas were informed by the seemingly fixed nature of sex and biology, as well as by contemporary gender expectations, biases and exclusions. Hurston was an adult before women received the right to vote in 1920 with the passage of the Nineteenth Amendment. She lived 65 of her 69 years under Jim Crow. For additional context here, it is helpful to turn to bell hooks, who, 'in a retrospective examination of the black female slave experience', argued that 'sexism looms as large as racism as an oppressive force in the lives of black women.'[29]

Institutionalized sexism – that is, patriarchy – formed the base of the American social structure along with racial imperialism. Sexism was an integral part of the social and political order white colonizers brought with them from their European homelands, and it was to have a grave impact on the fate of enslaved black women.[30]

It is clear that despite her poverty, and in accordance with her life and work, Hurston in 1941 – while finishing up the manuscript of her autobiography – considered herself to be among the strong rather than the weak of mankind. She wrote from the perspective and with the spirit of a frontierswoman – someone accustomed to seeking out their fortune in new lands, who values self-reliance and adheres to the idea of a strong work ethic, strength of person and character. Moreover, she worked as a woman whose bold behaviour was in opposition to the status quo.

Dust Tracks might be said to presage Hurston's novel *Seraph on the Suwanee*, the first of her novels to centre white Southerners. Set on the Suwanee River in northwest Florida, Hurston's final published novel marked a shift in subject for the seasoned writer. *Seraph* is not set in Hurston's now familiar all-Black Florida town of Eatonville but rather due north, near Jacksonville, in a river-based town. Instead of the pear tree of *Their Eyes Were Watching God*, there is the sheltering mulberry tree, or 'a cool green temple of peace', of Arvay Henson's impoverished and disrupted childhood.[31] The central characters in the novel are Southern white Americans, characters whose socioeconomic powers shift during the course of the book and whose access to wealth is fostered by a political, economic and labour system rigged in their favour.

The novel centres on the courtship and marriage of the low-born Arvay and Jim Meserve, a mill worker with limited means, a dream and a family name. Although neither Jim nor Arvay have much when growing up, neither of them starts out in abject poverty; as such, this is not a 'rags to riches' story. Most compellingly, Hurston foregrounds the white sexual politics of the time (the early to mid-twentieth century), a heterosexual politics both shaped and delimited by materiality: in this case, for Southern white characters born to the labouring class, and who become part of the elite class. A notable aspect of Jim and Arvay's courtship and subsequent marriage is the silence at its centre. Their relationship is sexual before they even communicate: Jim rapes Arvay, taking her virginity, and then he all but forces her to marry him, despite her protestations. As the scholar Chris Roark writes, 'During their first extended meeting, when Jim escorts Arvay to church and then home, he responds directly to her resistance, "But you might as well save yourself a whole heap of trouble in that line, Miss Arvay, because I'm going to marry you first and last."'[32] Not only is he determined to marry Arvay, against her wishes, Jim is also determined to have sex with Arvay regardless of her willingness.

When Jim rapes Arvay, he establishes a dynamic for their sexual and nonsexual relationship as husband and wife. That is, as Adrienne Akins argues, 'Jim's violent exercise of [sexual and physical] power defines' his and Arvay's relationship, 'giving [Jim's] subsequent actions [that is, he still marries her] the appearance of kindness despite his own responsibility for the circumstances which cause Arvay to fear'.[33]

Arvay is compelled by Jim's sexual force, and forcing, so much so that she feels incapable of removing herself from him physically. Through the violence of his sexual violation of her, Jim marries himself sexually to Arvay, and soon legally marries her. The suggestion is that Arvay is addicted to sex with Jim as well as trapped in the marriage by her very addiction. As Boyd writes it, Arvay's 'life is defined by her marriage'.[34] Jim chooses Arvay and pursues her despite her wishes; though she resists Jim's advances, sexual and marital, this is to no avail. As a Southern white matriarch, or the metonymic figure of such, Arvay's defences always already fail against the capitalist-informed, white heteropatriarchy and ultimate supremacy of Jim – her husband, the father of her children and, Hurston suggests, her owner. In marrying Arvay and making her a wife and a mother, through rape and coercion, Jim Meserve depersonalizes her and renders her an object whose role is to please and serve him alone. As Boyd writes, Jim tells Arvay after the initial rape that she is '"going to keep on getting raped" for the rest of their life together'.[35] Arvay, who initially wanted to be a missionary and commit herself to God, is mocked by Jim who, in the words of Boyd, 'whoops': 'No more missionarying around for you. You done caught your heathen, baby.'[36] White heteropatriarchy wins at the novel's end. But so too does white matriarchy, for, as Akins argues, '*Seraph* indicates that Arvay's inferiority complex [in relation to Jim] is slowly replaced by a mindset that parallels Jim's own.'[37]

The couple do not speak openly or directly to one another until almost twenty years into their marriage, after the birth and raising of their three children, two boys and a girl. It is not until their children are grown and the couple have weathered several substantial storms, actual and figurative, that they 'reunite', so to speak. This takes place on Jim's first boat, which he names *Arvay Henson*. Jim is led by money, sex, comfort (at home) and order in accordance with his desire and will. The white matriarch, represented by Arvay, is both mother and whore. She coddles her husband even as she has sex with and submits to him, and as a result she is protected, well-housed and afforded sex and a 'respectable' sex life. It is through the character of Jim that Hurston shows the way that economic opportunity and solvency accords to white American businessmen in particular, and white men more generally. *Seraph* suggests that through selectivity and favour, technological progress, labour and determined strategizing, the wealth of men such as Jim grew, aided by the advent and entrenchment of the Jim Crow legal and cultural system then at play in the nation. That is, Jim is not exceptional, either in his efforts or his successes; he is just a white man. Charismatic, quick-witted and skilled, a man with gumption, Jim cannot help but achieve within a society primed for his success. White manhood all but guaranteed Jim property, businesses, a well-kept wife, well-educated children and generational economic solvency.

In Hurston's foregrounding of white economic supremacy in tandem with a legally sanctioned white political, cultural and legal supremacy, the systemic become endemic. What is believed to be the 'natural order' of things is everywhere evident in the novel. In this way, Hurston makes explicit, and renders implicit, what would have been the status quo, simply the way of things, for her readers and critics alike at the time.

The sexual, emotional, economic and coercive violence at the centre of the Meserves' marriage – and thus their family, businesses and, suggests the novel, the larger white community – is in every way of low standing, and not by virtue of the fact that Avery was born into impoverished circumstances, or because Jim was originally a man with a name but limited means. Hurston finds both her white characters and the larger white society they represent to be limited and lacking. Hurston heralds Martin Luther King Jr's assertion that it is the content of one's character and not one's

Hurston in 1948. This photograph was part of the promotional material for her novel *Seraph on the Suwanee*, the only one of Hurston's novels to centre on white Southerners. Hurston looks elegant, and every bit the established author.

pocketbook (or wallet) that determines their worth. Neither the Meserves' race nor their rising socio-economic status can rescue or recuse them from the judgement of a Creator, that is, Hurston, who has known, seen and imagined better. Ultimately, both Jim and Arvay prove themselves to be suspect as characters, and as such call into question contemporaneous notions of Southern white Americans as a chosen or elite group.

As in earlier novels by Hurston, it is possible to read her own biography into its details. For example, the two sisters at the centre, one of whom is favoured and the other disfavoured by the father, may be read as Sarah and Zora Neale Hurston, respectively. More directly, perhaps, we might read some of the Hurston family's biography in the novel and the story of the Meserves. That is, might *Seraph* be read as a reverse or inverted telling of John and Lucy Hurston and their children's story – the Hurston family story in whiteface? One could argue that Jim Meserve is a doppelganger and double of John Hurston as much as Arvay Henson is a doppelganger of Lucy Potts. In both instances, the wife is subject to the demands and whims of the husband-patriarch.

7

The Dulling Final Years

In a letter of 1950 to the poet Carl Sandburg, Hurston writes, 'I am an anthropologist and it is my job to see and to find and present to the world my findings. I have seen extracts from *Mules and Men* printed in many languages, proving that I did a fairly good job.'[1] Hurston continues that she 'never expected to get rich' and that if she 'served this nation and the world by digging out a few of it's [*sic*] hidden treasures and thus enriched our culture, I have gained a great deal'.[2] In a letter from the same year to her friend Sara Lee Creech, Hurston writes of the

> conclusion that I have reached some years ago from observation. That is, that the so-called Race Problem will be solved in the South and by Southerners. I have noted that when a Southerner becomes convinced, he goes all out for correcting the situation. I need not cite the numerous examples to a well-informed person like you.[3]

The woman writing in 1950 is well aware of her status, her calibre as a professional writer and simultaneously the very real material and psycho-social limitations of Jim Crow society. Hurston knows she has left an indelible mark on her nation and culture, and that despite her success, wealth was never an expectation or a guarantee. This is a woman sharp in mind and deliberate; a woman who clearly, and rightly, sees Sandburg as a colleague and a contemporary (and, it would seem, one willing to lend an ear).

Wealthy or not, in thirty years, Hurston had established herself as a leading voice in African American literature, art and culture, as well as helped to foment the study of working or peasant-class African Americans. Alice Walker writes that 'implicit in Hurston's determination to "make it" in a career was her need to express "the folk" and herself'.[4] Walker continues, 'Someone who knew her has said: "Zora would have been Zora even if she'd been an Eskimo." That is what it means to be yourself; it is surely what it means to be an artist.' Walker adds further, invoking a renowned Blues singer and Black woman of Hurston's generation, 'Bessie Smith knew shit when she saw it, and from Zora Hurston's work, we can assume she did too.'[5] For Walker, Hurston's work of 'writing down the unwritten doings and sayings of a culture nobody else seemed to give a damn about, except to wish it would more rapidly conform to white, middle-class standards' is but one measure of just how much she 'knew shit when she saw it'.[6] She was 'made of some of the universe's most naturally free stuff (one would be hard pressed to find a more nonmaterialistic person), was denied even a steady pittance, free from strings, that would have kept her secure enough to do her best work'.[7] Hurston died 'still following *her* vision and *her* road'.[8] Walker adds further, 'That Hurston held her own, literally, against the flood of whiteness and maleness that diluted so much other black art of the period in which she worked is a testimony to her genius and her faith.'[9]

Hurston did quite a bit more living and doing in the years between 1950, when she returned to Florida to live – for good this time – and 1960, when she died. Hurston had lived on houseboats between the years 1943 and 1947; sea living and water living had allowed her far more freedom of movement in the Jim Crow U.S. South. In 1947 she set sail to Honduras after receiving a $300 advance from Scribner's for *Seraph on the Suwanee*, and remained there through December, after a second advance, revising the novel. Although Eatonville was her city and is the topography for much of her fiction, Hurston claimed the entire state of Florida as home. She lived variously in Jacksonville, Eau Gallie, Plant City, Longwood, Eatonville, St Augustine, Daytona Beach and, for long stretches, Miami. Hurston seems to have favoured the southeast and coastal parts of the state.

By 1950, Hurston had been 'written out'.[10] She became a resident of Belle Glade, Florida, following a stint as a maid on wealthy Rivo Alto Island in Miami. Hurston had taken the job to make money while she wrote, but news that she, a famous writer, was working as a maid of course made headlines. On 27 March 1950 the *Miami Herald* published an expose on Hurston, entitled 'Famous Negro Author Working as a Maid Here Just "to Live a Little"'.[11] Following this exposure, Hurston left her job and Miami, and went to work for George A. Smathers, a Florida conservative who was running for and won his bid for senator. Soon after, Hurston was hired by Smathers's father, a retired judge, as a ghost writer for his memoir.[12] 'After only a couple of months', writes Boyd, Hurston '"escaped" from the employ of the irascible old judge'.[13] Boyd continues, 'With his Old South background and beliefs, Smathers "could not accept the reality that a descendant of slaves could do something in an intellectual way that he could not".'[14] Hurston quit the job and headed to New York, where she spent the autumn catching up with old acquaintances before returning to Florida, where she would remain until her death.

Hurston moved to Belle Glade so that she could live 'with friends', with the hope of saving money.[15] She also bought a used car for the express purpose of touring the Everglades. Hurston was then working on a novel, a manuscript about the first self-made African American woman millionaire, Madam C. J. Walker, which Hurston had titled 'The Golden Bench of God' (the novel was never finished). Hurston and Walker had crossed paths during Hurston's early years in New York in the 1920s. In 1950 Hurston was 59 years old. She craved her own space and was 'desperately hoping to sell a piece of writing soon so she could afford her own place'.[16] Shortly after her relocation, Hurston was moving again, this time to Eau Gallie, where she would make a home for herself for six years. In Eau Gallie, Hurston rented 'for $5 a week the same one-room cabin she had lived in when finishing *Mules and Men*'.[17] She transformed the shoddy cabin into a home where she planted and tended a vegetable and flower garden. Hurston grew pole beans and sold whatever surplus she had. She grew oleanders and gardenias, and she wrote.

The beauty of Hurston's gardens attracted 'sightseers'.[18] Hurston kept the interior of her cabin simple. Always present were her typewriter, her desk and her chair. Maybe there was a vase of azaleas brought in from her flower garden; surely there was a water glass. This was perhaps the longest stable living space and environment Hurston was to have had since her girlhood. Hurston made the tiny cabin over, 'happily repairing [the] house' and clearing the land to plant her gardens.[19]

Hurston 'lived contentedly in Eau Gallie', where she began but 'never finished' a sequel to *Dust Tracks on the Road*.[20] Hurston also submitted to and had rejected by her publisher, Scribner's, the unpublished manuscript for 'The Golden Bench of God'. She published 'A Negro Voter Sizes Up Taft' in the *Saturday Evening Post*, which Wall writes was 'a favourable profile of Ohio Senator Robert Taft, a leading candidate for the 1952 Republican presidential nomination'.[21] Hurston also wrote 'stories about her pet dog Spot, adapt[ed] biblical tales, research[ed] articles on Florida cattle and colonialism in Southeast Asia, and consider[ed] writing about career women returning to work in the home'.[22] But Hurston faced 'increasing difficulty selling her work'.[23]

During her time in Eau Gallie, in the early 1950s, Hurston also gave 'five folk concerts in six weeks to earn money'; she reported on 'the trial of Ruby McCollum, a black woman charged with the murder of a prominent white doctor who had been her lover' for the *Pittsburgh Courier*. According to Wall, Hurston's articles defending Ruby appeared in the *Courier* from 11 October 1952 to 2 May 1953.'[24] Despite her defence in the media, Ruby was sentenced to death, but 'after the sentence was overturned on appeal, she was declared mentally incompetent and committed to a state hospital where she remained for 20 years.'[25] In addition to this, Hurston began work on 'a biography of Herod the Great, a project she . . . contemplated for years' and whom Hurston considered to be 'a great soldier, statesman, and lover'; it would be a book Hurston hoped would appeal to producers in Hollywood.[26] Although the book, too, would be rejected by Scribner's, this was a rich period for Hurston – in simple terms, she was producing work and her living conditions were suitable. It was during this period that Hurston also wrote and had published a letter critical of the U.S. Supreme Court case *Brown v. Board of Education*, which had declared segregation in schools based on race to be unconstitutional. Hurston was critical of 'the Court's implication that black children could learn only when they went to school with whites'.[27] Hurston's letter was 'widely reprinted in southern newspapers and produce[d] a sensation that surprise[d] Hurston and anger[d] civil-rights leaders'.[28]

In March 1956 Hurston received an eviction notice 'from her landlord, who [was] selling the house'. Her cabin's relative closeness to the water coupled with her upkeep made the place prime real estate. Once again, Hurston was being made to leave her home. This time, however, she was not a girl, not a child, but rather an accomplished, successful – though still poor – writer and scholar. She could take care of herself, as she always had. Kaplan writes that when Hurston was evicted 'she seemed at loose ends', but left the cabin in early spring.[29] She took 'a job in June as library clerk at Patrick Air Force Base in Cocoa Beach, Florida'.[30] She was 'paid $1.88 an hour for filing technical literature' and hated it, and left the job after eleven months.[31] Hemenway writes that Hurston's time working at the air force base made her 'eligible for unemployment, and she found that she could just make it on the twenty-six dollars per week'.[32]

In 1958, at the age of 67, Hurston was hired by 'C. E. Bolen, publisher of the *Fort Pierce Chronicle*, a local black newspaper' and relocated to Fort Pierce, where she supplemented 'her unemployment checks with freelance fees from Bolen's' paper and by writing a column, 'Hoodoo and Black Magic'.[33] Kaplan writes that Hurston was 'taking a step down for a woman who had written for many nationally prominent magazines and papers, including *The Pittsburgh Courier, Opportunity,* and *Saturday Evening Post, Negro Digest, Story, American Mercury,* and *Saturday Evening Post*'.[34] Kaplan continues that 'Hurston had not worked as a regular journalist, so by accepting Bolen's offer she was taking up the responsibility of starting a new career; in ill health, broke, and at sixty-years of age.'[35]

Hurston would live just three more years. By February 1958 Hurston was 'substitute teaching at Lincoln Park Academy, the

segregated black public school of Fort Pierce'.[36] Hemenway writes
that Hurston 'was not very successful [in the job] and had several
run-ins with students'.[37] In Fort Pierce, Hurston 'lived in a house
owned by her physician, Dr. C. C. Benton, at 1734 School Court
Street'.[38] As with her cabin in Eau Gallie, Hurston 'made the tiny,
bare yard' of her Fort Pierce home 'bloom', growing 'azaleas,
morning glories, and gardenias'.[39] She also 'put in a vegetable
garden to raise collards and tomatoes [and] labored on the Herod
manuscript'.[40] According to Benton, Hurston 'was always studying.
Her mind . . . just worked all the time.'[41]

Hurston's poverty exacerbated her lifelong health issues,
and she began to hold weight on her body in ways she had not
before. Hurston was 'increasingly plagued by health problems,
including a tropical virus contracted from impure drinking water
in Honduras, [a] gall bladder infection, [an] irritated colon, and the
effects of obesity'.[42] Her ageing body and her poor diet, a result of

Zora's home in Fort Pierce, Florida, 1958 or 1959. Hurston's age and economic poverty
are evident.

limited food options and access, compounded by lifelong stomach problems, meant that, physically speaking, the opening years of Hurston's sixties were often uncomfortable. Her health continued to decline with age. Still, Hurston was putting fingers to typewriter keys and writing.

According to reports, the last decade or so of Hurston's life (the years 1948 to 1959) were perhaps her most challenging. The year 1948 marked a nadir for Hurston. In February, she was accused of molesting a young boy. Although there was scant evidence and Hurston was in Honduras doing field research at the time the assault was said to have taken place, Hurston was still charged and jailed. Hurston's white elite friends came to her rescue, providing bail and a place for Hurston to lay low and recover from the trauma of the case. Once the Black press caught wind of her jailing and ran with the story, seeking little, if any, factual evidence, and despite the fact that the case was subsequently dropped and Hurston exonerated, she was never able to recover her career and reputation. There were those who simply refused to believe, despite all evidence, that Hurston was innocent. In response to what she experienced as betrayal (the court stenographer who took the story to the press was also African American), Hurston turned away from the very people she laboured, both as folklorist and as a writer, to celebrate, render complex and whole – her own Black people.

Although Hurston wrote non-stop, she struggled thereafter to secure a publisher for her work. Hurston increasingly turned to journalism, which helped pay the bills. Like any sane and world-weary person, Hurston also turned inwards. As Washington notes, Hurston's final decade proved 'a difficult time' for the novelist, 'mainly because she had very little money and few means of self-support other than her writing, which was not going well'.[43] Hurston's health was ailing, and she proved ill-equipped for daytime jobs, most of which would have been beneath her standing.

In her last years, living in Fort Pierce, Hurston worked as a librarian, journalist and, for some time, an elementary school teacher. Hurston died in poverty and relative obscurity. Significantly, for her Black American culture, as a funeral attendee put it about Hurston, 'She didn't come to you empty.'[44] Still, by the time of her death, Hurston was tired, written out, and yet still writing with the hope of publishing. Furthermore, she was attempting to pour much of what she knew into the children in her neighbourhood, encouraging them all to write and to keep a journal.

Hurston died at 7 p.m., 'an hour past sundown', on 28 January 1960 following a stroke.[45] As Boyd writes, Zora 'died "in poverty"'.[46] Donations came from 'both Lippincott and Scribner's' in the amount of $100. The novelists Carl Van Vechten and Fanny Hurst sent funds to aid in Hurston's burial, as did 'a group of Hurston's former students', who contributed what they had in the amount of $2.50. Donations for the funeral amounted to $661.87, and 'the undertaker donated the burial plot'.[47] Although Hurston was buried in an unmarked grave in Fort Pierce, Florida, in 1990 Lucy Hurston Hogan, Hurston's niece, authorized 'that [Hurston's] remains be moved to Eatonville'.[48]

At 69 years old, Hurston, according to Boyd, had 'lived three years longer than the average . . . black American woman was expected to live'.[49] Hurston's funeral was held on 7 February, and was deemed 'impressive'.[50] One funeral attendee said of Hurston, 'Zora Neale went about and didn't care too much how she looked. Or what she said. Maybe people didn't think so much of that. But Zora Neale, every time she went about, had something to offer.'[51] Hemenway writes that the minister overseeing Hurston's funeral service followed with, 'They said she couldn't become a writer recognized by the world. But she did it. The Miami paper said she died poor. But she died rich. She did something.'[52] Indeed. Zora Neale Hurston's life, and especially her creativity, intellectualism, writing and work on behalf of Black life and Black culture, as well as on the part of Black American artistic and literary productions, serve as testament to this fact. Hurston's legacy as a writer, artist and intellectual continues.

Epilogue: 'I'm Not Done Yet'

We were not supposed to know of a Zora Neale Hurston, a Black woman writer born in the nineteenth century and who came to prominence as a professional anthropologist and folklorist with extensive experience in the field. We were not supposed to know of this now world-renowned Southern-born Black woman novelist who grew up among the labouring classes but was from a land-owning and home-owning two-parent family, and who was the fifth of her parents' eight children. As the contemporary scholar and theorist Tressie McMillan Cottom writes in *Thick: And Other Essays* (2019), 'prestige, money, and power structure our so-called democratic institutions so that most of us' – and this is especially true, she argues, for Black women – 'will always fail'.[1] She continues, 'as objectified superhumans, we are valuable. As humans, we are incompetent.'[2] And yet we know Zora Neale Hurston's life – what we are able to know of it – and we know her critical and creative work.

Hurston was born a Black girl in the Deep South, less than a decade after Reconstruction ended and Black Americans were essentially left by the government to fend for themselves. She was born in a virulently violent, white-supremacist former slavocracy. Like her parents before her, it would seem, Hurston jumped at the sun, keeping her eye on a far-better imaged and imagined horizon. When Hurston's family relocated from Alabama to Eatonville, Florida, when she was an infant, they perhaps inadvertently bequeathed their daughter a legacy of nomadism, as well as one of questing after and going in the direction of sunlight – Zora made of herself a woman, a persona, a spirit and a creative sensibility that

Hurston, 30 April 1956, at the age of 65. At the time she was living in Eau Gallie, Florida, which existed as an independent city from 1860 to 1969 before merging with the neighbouring Melbourne. Many of the city's residents were, like Hurston, African American.

was, in her own words, 'drenched in light'.[3] For those who could see it, Hurston radiated light. She was a smart, adept child, a quick learner and a gifted reader and storyteller. But you had to be able and willing to see her light, and not everyone was – especially when Hurston was a child but also throughout her life. She was a Black woman doing what few Black women – or women full stop – did. She made her way in the world by her own mind and hand, with the assistance of a charisma and insouciance that either drew one to her or served to put a wall up between Hurston and themselves.

Hurston was operating in what was considered the masculine space of the public world in the 1920s and '30s. She was doing so not only as an often single woman – thus as one not legitimized through her association with a man – but often without regard for gendered and, to a degree, racialized expectations and norms. Hurston was herself, yes; but she was also altered by her close association with elite white Americans who held economic sway and power over her and her work. This began with her first extended stay away from the all-Black Eatonville when she was sent off to school at the age of thirteen. Hurston never did develop a love for the city of Jacksonville. She could never 'cut it down to size', which suggests that at thirteen, travelling alone in a Jim Crow South, the sense of being overwhelmed must have been profound – and it clearly marked her.[4] Hurston waitressed at the elite Cosmos Club in Washington, DC, an all-male, primarily white club catering to leading male figures in the humanities. What sort of conversations and exchanges would have occurred between Hurston and these reified men? What interchanges occurred between Hurston as a manicurist and the elite, powerful white men in DC politics she buffed and catered to, in a Black-owned barbershop that was for white customers only? What must it have felt like to daily experience being the first African American student to graduate from Barnard College?

After Hurston's mother passed away and her father remarried and turned away, Zora, at fourteen years old, lived a life that few but Hurston, and perhaps those she lived among, knew about. Hurston kept silent on the decade following her mother's death, 1904 to 1914, a period in which it is believed she may have been subject to rape, domestic partner violence and periods of indigence and hunger. Valerie Boyd writes,

> From the time she was a little girl, dogged by clairvoyant visions of her future, Zora knew that (in her words) 'a house, a shot-gun built house that needed a new coat of white paint, held torture for me, but I must go. I saw deep love betrayed, but I must feel and know it. There was no turning back.'[5]

By 1914 or 1915, Hurston arrived at this foreseen house and lived to tell about it, but she never spoke of the period.[6] As Kaplan explains, little is known about the years immediately following Hurston's mother's death, except that 'they were difficult'.[7] As a consequence, 'Hurston's teen years, from 1905 to 1912 . . . are often known as "the missing decade" or the "lost years," years Hurston hid by changing her age and by revealing nothing from that time period.'[8] We can speculate about what may have happened to Hurston during those ten formative years of her teens and early adulthood. However, perhaps it would behove us to take Hurston's lead and recognize that, in the words of Alice Walker, 'One's experience, in fact, is all one ever truly owns.'[9] Hurston was close-mouthed as a way of keeping her sense of herself as whole, human and free – which is to say she had a whole intact 'inside self' that was and would remain hers alone.

At 26 years old, Hurston had aged out of a free education as an American citizen, and in particular as a Florida-reared, African American woman born just fifteen years after Reconstruction officially ended in the U.S. South. Hurston was youthful in appearance, smart, charismatic as always, and determined. Though others such as the Black woman writer Dorothy West would suspect Hurston was older than she stated, Hurston seemed willing and able to take on the life and persona of a woman ten years younger than her actual age, from 1916 onwards. Photographs of her at 28 years old masquerading as eighteen 'show' a young Black woman of the early 1920s with knowing eyes and a wry smile, and do little to suggest her actual age.

Hurston could in fact be an eighteen-year-old, one thinks when looking at images of her taken by her former sweetheart, and one of her three husbands, Herbert Sheen, during their time together at Howard University in 1921. It was at Howard that Hurston would meet Alain Locke, the philosopher who in 1925 would publish *The New Negro*, the first collection to showcase the new art of those contemporary Black writers who would become the vanguard of the Harlem Renaissance, pointing the way for the bourgeoning Black Arts Movement of the 1960s. Though Locke was unaware of it when he noticed the talent of what he took to be the young, budding writer, he and Hurston were but a few years apart in age.

Hurston's grades varied depending on her interest in the subject. However, her commitment to securing an education never flagged. When Locke took notice of Hurston in 1920–21, he was taking in a woman who had lived; who had loved and lost both her parents and been dispersed and separated from her siblings; a woman who had perhaps committed herself to an abusive and demoralizing man whom she had to escape; and a woman who supported herself by occasional work as a maid and other forms of labour available to Black women in the South in the first decades of the 1900s.

While Hurston was not the Harvard- and Oxford-educated scholar Locke was, he recognized in his then student her talent as a writer and a thinker; and, as literary and cultural history and herstory show, Locke and Hurston were well matched. Hurston's love of trains (which she shared with her father and with her first character, John Pearson); her need of and appreciation for her cars, such as 'Sassy Susie' and her 1939 red convertible; and her purchase of, living on and travel by houseboats all point to her positioning as a late nineteenth- and early twentieth-century subject compelled by, and putting to use, contemporaneous advances in technology. Modern technological developments, especially the automobile and the typewriter, would bode well for Hurston in that such advances, and her relative access to them, allowed a greater, more expansive life for this born-curious first-nighter.

In my 2013 essay titled 'Zora Neale Hurston as Womanist', published in *Critical Insights: Zora Neale Hurston* (2013), I argued that Hurston was living 'womanism' long before Alice Walker coined the term to mean 'a black feminist or a feminist of color'.[10] (This is not the same as saying that Hurston was a womanist or a feminist but rather that she had her ways, as we say in the U.S. South.) As a scholar of motherhood whose work primarily focuses on disruptions in the Black mother–daughter relationship, I was eager to get my hands and thoughts on Hurston, or 'Mama's child'.[11] I was primed for her sleight of hand with respect to the age she proffered when her mother died. There are significant differences between a girl of nine, the age Hurston gives in her autobiography, and a girl of thirteen, Hurston's actual age when her mother passed. Thirteen-year-old Black girls during Hurston's childhood would have been regarded by white and Black Americans alike as sexually lascivious, and thus as a sexual threat. She would have been ostracized by many, not embraced as perhaps a girl of nine, albeit African American, might have. That is Hurston's power as a writer: she can affect the consciousness of her reader, and by extension the ideas and narratives her readers put out in the world about her as a woman bent on keeping private what is none of our business. Hurston was an amalgam of the modern woman, the New Woman and the New Negro.

Hurston's tone in much of her writing, whether fiction or non-fiction, often belied the fact that the novelist and anthropologist was in a constant state of anxiety. She wrote constantly, unless unable to due to lethargy or exhaustion, and was always concerned about money and negotiating often challenging relationships with patrons. Family and interfamilial relations form the backdrop of her creative aesthetic and psyche and inform all other relationships, whether personal or professional, in which Hurston engages. Though known to disappear, most likely for the purposes of writing and also perhaps to skate the ever-present judgement of her life, work and choices, Hurston was always available to her family, and she remained until her last days a beloved aunt to her two nieces, whom she helped to care for in her teenage years, as well as to her nephew, Edward Jr, her baby brother's son and perhaps Hurston's favourite of all her siblings' children.

People tend to render pathological what they do not understand – or, what we refuse to understand or even acknowledge as valid and human. Hurston understood most readily that U.S. society has never been amenable to Black life. Black women's lives, even less so. Hurston became the most published Black woman writer during the first half of the twentieth century in the United States. That was in the very nation that previously enslaved her father, maternal grandmother and generations of her family and non-family alike. Hurston's father was a leading Baptist minister, and her mother was Mother of the Church as well as a Sunday school teacher. This means that Hurston's parents were leaders in their community even on the level of the personal and the religious. I offer this insight as a woman from a Holiness background who, although having stepped away from the faith, recognizes the impact that that particular upbringing continues to have on my life and choices.

Hurston was raised on the Old Testament, in which God's vengeance is evident and man's errors and ways are ever present and borderline maddening (for this reader, as they surely were for the Christian God of the Bible). Hurston was a contradiction: nontraditional in many ways yet traditional in others. She valued men and marriage, but she did not concede to submitting or sublimating herself to a man in marriage. Her work was her priority over the marriages and love affairs. Hurston was upfront about the importance of securing her life through her ability to secure an education and to make a living. In *Dust Tracks on a Road*, she responds to a young Black man's integrationist attempt to desegregate the Black-owned, whites-only barbershop in which she worked when at Howard with what reads as disdain: this is because Hurston understands capitalism, and she was far from delusional about the United States as an apartheid nation. One might say she lacked faith in a nation she claimed to love; or we could go further and seek to understand the United States from Hurston's, and surely her father's, complex perspective.

Hurston was criticized during her time and, it would seem, dismissed for decades because of what others deemed her

Hurston demonstrating her love of contemporary fashion and perhaps signifying 19th-century portraiture of middle-class and elite African Americans in her own 20th-century modernist and New Negro/New Woman way. Her smile, posture and dress – not to mention the ukulele – seem to modernize contemporaneous tropes of Black portraiture.

minstrel-like performances with white patrons, her particular and personal politics and her art, which was reflective of the woman herself – bold, intriguing and at times taboo, and thus needed. We know today the enormous challenges faced by Hurston in particular, and by Black women, famous and not, more generally. We know as well that every action and speech pattern is in some way a performance. The actor Lincoln 'Stepin Fetchit' Perry was able to make a living and retire from his profession. Hurston continues to be criticized in language both vague and concrete to this day. Just how much do we as a society, nation and world culture value and devalue Black women?

Hurston belonged to the second generation of Black Americans born free on her maternal side, and the first generation of Black

Americans born free on her paternal side. Thus when Hurston writes in her famous 1928 essay that she does not 'belong to that sobbing school of Negrohood who hold that nature has somehow given them a lowdown dirty deal and whose feelings are all hurt about it' owing to the fact that she is African American, she is both being jocular and emphatic.[12] Her conception of Blackness, and of Black American identity, was affirming, informed by her experiences as a trained social scientist and most of all by her valuation and love of Black people and Black culture. This love, and the value that Hurston saw in Black America, shows the influence of family, society and culture. Hurston believed in personal dignity. It is essential to let that idea register and settle. It is an affront to one's dignity, to one's sense of self as whole, to submit to an idea of oneself or race as pathological, reduced and a result of the pressures and oppressions of another. As a woman, Hurston had little tolerance for personal weakness. She ran towards what she desired and away from what she did not. She had a penchant for young, beautiful, intelligent and dark-skinned Black men with 'bright soul[s], a fine mind in a fine body, and courage', as she writes in *Dust Tracks on a Road*.[13] She liked and benefited from the friendship of gutsy, determined white and Black women, most of whom struggled with aspects of their past, their girlhood. Fannie Hurst, the novelist for whom Hurston worked, though wealthy, was lonely as a child. To compensate, she played games with herself, which she continued into adulthood. The famous blues singer and stage performer Ethel Waters, whom Hurston befriended in the 1930s, had a troubled past. For her, religion was a salve. When Hurston was with Waters, she could sit and think. The two talked as intimates, and Hurston must have found in her a mother figure. How Hurston loved and missed her mother Lucy, lost to her when she was merely thirteen years old. Where does all that childhood longing for a mother go? For Hurston, it manifested in her relationship with others. What Boyd regards as her continuous search for a partner, the other half of an incomplete whole, I regard as a search for communion, a seeking out of the self in others.

Hurston was 'the recipient of two Guggenheims and the author of four novels, a dozen short stories, two musicals, two

Hurston at 48 years old sitting on a porch at a turpentine camp in Cross City, Florida, in 1939.

books on black mythology, dozens of essays, and a prizewinning autobiography'.[14] Still, for 'three full decades', writes Henry Louis Gates Jr, she 'virtually "disappear[ed]" from her readership'.[15] He adds, 'the loving, diverse, and enthusiastic responses that Hurston's work engenders today were not shared by her black male contemporaries.'[16] Gates notes that Hurston also published 'more than fifty shorter works between the middle of the Harlem

Renaissance and the end of the Korean War, when she was the dominant black woman writer in the United States'.[17] However, she was 'virtually ignored after the early fifties, even by the Black Arts movement in the sixties'.[18] In this way, argues Gates, Hurston defies 'glib categories of "radical" or "conservative", "black" or "Negro", "revolutionary" or "Uncle Tom"', which are 'categories of little use in literary criticism' or indeed in criticism more generally.[19]

What Hurston wanted more than wealth, more perhaps than fame, was 'peace and quiet to sit down and try to learn how to write in truth', as she had 'always been too hurried before'.[20] Hurston created and fostered a life for herself that allowed for the creation of art, and she made lasting contributions to the fields of literature, autobiography, cultural studies, folklore and anthropology. What she left behind, in terms of both her writing and her approach to living, continues to inspire, inform and generate new art, literature and insights into the African American experience and its culture, as well as into professional, creative Black women's art and lived realities.

References

Introduction

1 Zora Neale Hurston, letter to Henry Allen Moe, 5 May 1936, in *Zora Neale Hurston: A Life in Letters*, ed. Carla Kaplan (New York, 2002), p. 376.
2 Hurston, letter to William Pickens, 1917/18, in *A Life in Letters*, ed. Kaplan, p. 54.
3 Hurston, letter to Annie Nathan Meyer, 12 May 1925, in *A Life in Letters*, ed. Kaplan, p. 55.
4 Ibid.
5 bell hooks, *Yearning: Race, Gender, and Cultural Politics*, 2nd edn (New York, 2013), p. 135.

1 Childhood

1 Cheryl A. Wall, ed., *Zora Neale Hurston, Novels and Stories: Jonah's Gourd Vine/ Their Eyes Were Watching God/ Moses, Man of the Mountain/ Seraph on the Suwanee/ Selected Stories* (Washington, DC, 1995), p. 1013. In her 'Chronology' section, Wall puts forward that Hurston's given name at birth was Zora Lee Hurston. In Zora Neale Hurston, *Dust Tracks on a Road* (New York, 1942), p. 21, Hurston suggests that 'Lee' became 'Neale' a day after her birth, when 'a Mrs. Neale, a friend of Mama's[,] came in and reminded her that she had promised to let her name the baby in case it was a girl . . . so I became "Zora Neale Hurston"'.
2 Ann R. Morris and Margaret M. Dunn, 'Flora and Fauna in Hurston's Florida Novels', in *Zora in Florida*, ed. Steve Glassman and Kathryn Lee Seidel (Orlando, FL, 1991), p. 2.

3 Ibid.

4 Zora Neale Hurston, 'Drenched in Light', in *Zora Neale Hurston, Novels and Stories*, ed. Wall (Washington, DC, 1995), pp. 940–48.

5 Hurston, *Dust Tracks on a Road*, p. 71.

6 Ibid.

7 Valerie Boyd, *Wrapped in Rainbows: The Life of Zora Neale Hurston* (New York, 2003), p. 55.

8 Zora Neale Hurston, 'How It Feels to Be Colored Me', in *I Love Myself When I Am Laughing: A Zora Neale Hurston Reader*, ed. Alice Walker (New York, 2011), p. 152.

9 Darlene Clark Hine, William C. Hine and Stanley Harrold, *The African-American Odyssey* (New York, 2017), pp. 380–95.

10 Ibid., p. 382.

11 Ibid.

12 Hurston, 'How It Feels to Be Colored Me', p. 154.

13 Ibid., p. 151.

14 Ibid.

15 Ibid.

16 Ibid.

17 Esther Newton, 'The Mythic Mannish Lesbian: Radclyffe Hall and the New Woman', *Signs*, IX/4 (1984), pp. 557–75.

18 Ibid., p. 562.

19 Hurston, *Dust Tracks on a Road*, p. 68.

20 Patricia Hill Collins, *Black Feminist Thought: Knowledge, Consciousness, and the Politics of Empowerment* (Abingdon, 1999), p. 231.

2 Opportunity

1 Yuval Taylor, *Zora and Langston: A Story of Friendship and Betrayal* (New York, 2019), p. 33.

2 To read the poem in its entirety, see the 2004 interactive collection *Speak, So You Can Speak Again: The Life of Zora Neale Hurston* (New York, 2004), a work edited by Hurston's niece, Lucy Anne Hurston, a writer-scholar and representative of the Estate of Zora Neale Hurston.

3 Ibid., p. 9.

4 Ibid.

5 Zora Neale Hurston, 'How It Feels to Be Colored Me', in *I Love Myself When I Am Laughing: A Zora Neale Hurston Reader*, ed. Alice Walker (New York, 2011), p. 152.

6 Zora Neale Hurston, 'John Redding Goes to Sea', in *Zora Neale Hurston, Novels and Stories: Jonah's Gourd Vine/ Their Eyes Were Watching God/ Moses, Man of the Mountain/ Seraph on the Suwanee/ Selected Stories*, ed. Cheryl A. Wall (Washington, DC, 1995), pp. 925–39.

7 Ibid.

8 Ibid.

9 Ibid., p. 939.

10 Ibid., p. 925.

11 Ibid., p. 933.

12 Ibid., pp. 933–4.

13 Robert Hemenway, *Zora Neale Hurston: A Literary Biography* (Urbana, IL, 1977), p. 84.

14 Hurston writes of Carl Van Vechten in *Dust Tracks on a Road* (New York, 1942), pp. 268–9: 'If he is your friend, he will point out your failings as well as your good points in the most direct manner. Take it or leave it . . . but he is as true as the equator if he is for you.'

15 Warren J. Carson, 'Hurston as Dramatist: The Florida Connection', in *Zora in Florida*, ed. Steve Glassman and Kathryn Lee Seidel (Orlando, FL, 1991), p. 123.

16 Ibid., p. 124.

17 Ibid.

18 Ibid., p. 126.

19 Ibid.

20 Lucy Anne Hurston, ed., *Speak, So You Can Speak Again*, p. 15.

21 Ibid., pp. 15, 11.

22 Zora Neale Hurston, 'Spunk', in *Zora Neale Hurston: Novels and Stories*, ed. Wall, pp. 949–54, italics in original.

23 Ibid., p. 953.

24 Zora Neale Hurston, letter to Annie Nathan Meyer, 17 December 1925, in *Zora Neale Hurston: A Life in Letters*, ed. Carla Kaplan (New York, 2002), p. 72.

25 Ibid., p. 69.

26 Vernon J. Williams, *Rethinking Race: Franz Boas and His Contemporaries* (Lexington, KY, 1996), p. 167.

27 Valerie Smith, *Not Just Race, Not Just Gender: Black Feminist Readings* (New York and Abingdon, 2013), p. 64.

28 bell hooks, *Yearning: Race, Gender, and Cultural Politics*, 2nd edn (New York, 2013), p. 135.

29 Ibid.

30 Ibid.

31 Yuval Taylor, *Zora and Langston*, p. 141.

32 Ibid.

33 Ibid.

34 Ibid.

35 Hemenway, *A Literary Biography*, p. 123.

36 Mary Helen Washington, 'Zora Neale Hurston: A Woman Half in Shadow', in *I Love Myself When I Am Laughing*, ed. Walker, p. 9.

37 Ibid.

38 Ibid.

39 Hemenway, *A Literary Biography*, p. 160.

40 Hurston, 'How It Feels to Be Colored Me', p. 152.

3 Curiosity

1 Zora Neale Hurston, *Dust Tracks on a Road: An Autobiography* (New York, 1942), p. 204.

2 Ibid.

3 Ibid.

4 Zora Neale Hurston, letter to Langston Hughes, 8 March 1928, in *Zora Neale Hurston: A Life in Letters*, ed. Carla Kaplan (New York, 2002), p. 114.

5 Ibid.

6 See the Chronology in Zora Neale Hurston, *Novels and Stories: Jonah's Gourd Vine/ Their Eyes Were Watching God/ Moses, Man of the Mountain/ Seraph on the Suwanee/ Selected Stories*, ed. Cheryl A. Wall (Washington, DC, 1995), p. 1018.

7 Adrienne Brown, 'Hard Romping: Zora Neale Hurston, White Women, and the Right to Play', *Twentieth Century Literature*, LXIV/3 (September 2018), p. 310.

8 Yuval Taylor, *Zora and Langston: A Story of Friendship and Betrayal* (New York, 2019), p. 146.

9 Ibid., p. 147.

10 Ibid.

11 Ibid.

12 See 'Chronology', in *Zora Neale Hurston, Novels and Stories*, ed. Wall, p. 1018.

13 Zora Neale Hurston, 'How It Feels to Be Colored Me', in *I Love Myself When I Am Laughing: A Zora Neale Hurston Reader*, ed. Alice Walker (New York, 2011), pp. 151–4.

14 See Hurston, *Dust Tracks on a Road*, p. 14.
15 From Hurston, 'How It Feels to Be Colored Me', in *I Love Myself When I Am Laughing*, ed. Walker, p. 151.
16 Ibid., p. 153.
17 Ibid.
18 Carla Kaplan, *Zora Neale Hurston: A Life in Letters* (New York, 2002), p. 86.
19 Ibid.
20 Ibid.
21 Ibid.
22 Ibid.
23 Ibid., pp. 86, 85.
24 Ibid., p. 85.
25 Ibid., p. 86.
26 Ibid., p. 4.
27 Ibid.
28 Ibid., p. 171.
29 Ibid., p. 83.
30 Ibid.
31 Ibid., p. 84.
32 Ibid.
33 Mary Helen Washington, 'Zora Neale Hurston: A Woman Half in Shadow', in *I Love Myself When I Am Laughing*, ed. Walker, pp. 7–8.
34 Ibid.
35 Taylor, *Zora and Langston*, p. 139.
36 Zora Neale Hurston, letter to Franz Boas, 16 April 1930, in *A Life in Letters*, ed. Kaplan, p. 187.
37 Ibid.
38 Taylor, *Zora and Langston*, p. 88.
39 Zora Neale Hurston quoted in 'Chronology', ed. Wall, p. 1018.
40 Zora Neale Hurston, letter to Charlotte Osgood Mason, 18 May 1930.
41 Ibid., p. 189.
42 Ibid.
43 Brown, 'Hard Romping', p. 295.
44 Ibid., 296.
45 Ibid., p. 151
46 Hurston, 'How It Feels to Be Colored Me', p. 153.
47 Ibid.
48 Ibid.
49 Ibid.

50 Brown, 'Hard Romping', p. 297.

51 Hurston, 'How It Feels to Be Colored Me', p. 154.

52 Ibid., p. 152.

53 Ibid., p. 153.

54 Ibid.

55 Ibid., p. 154.

56 Ibid.

57 Ibid., p. 153.

58 Ibid.

4 On Fiction and Folklore

1 Valerie Boyd, *Wrapped in Rainbows: The Life of Zora Neale Hurston* (New York, 2003), p. 235.

2 Robert Hemenway, *Zora Neale Hurston: A Literary Biography* (Urbana, IL, 1977), p. 224.

3 Ibid.

4 Ibid.

5 Yuval Taylor, *Zora and Langston: A Story of Friendship and Betrayal* (New York, 2019), p. 4.

6 Beverly Guy-Sheftall, *Words of Fire: An Anthology of African American Feminist Thought* (New York, 1995), p. 77.

7 Henry Louis Gates Jr and Gene Andrew Jarrett, *The New Negro: Readings on Race, Representation, and African American Culture, 1892–1938* (Princeton, NJ, 2007), pp. 355–63.

8 Mary Helen Washington, 'Zora Neale Hurston: A Woman Half in Shadow', in *I Love Myself When I Am Laughing: A Zora Neale Hurston Reader*, ed. Alice Walker (New York, 2011), p. 9.

9 Zora Neale Hurston letter to Carl Van Vechten, 28 February 1934, in *Zora Neale Hurston: A Life in Letters*, ed. Carla Kaplan, (New York, 2002), p. 334.

10 Hemenway, *A Literary Biography*, p. 192.

11 Washington, 'A Woman Half in Shadow'.

12 Ibid.

13 Ibid.

14 Ibid.

15 Zora Neale Hurston, *Dust Tracks on a Road* (New York, 1942), p. 200.

16 Zora Neale Hurston, letter to Miguel Covarrubias, 31 January 1935, in *A Life in Letters*, ed. Kaplan, p. 290.

17 See Cheryl Hopson, 'The U.S. Women's Liberation Movement and Black Feminist "Sisterhood"', in *Provocations: A Transnational Reader in the History of Feminist Thought*, ed. Susan Bordo, M. Cristina Alcalde and Ellen Rosenman (Berkeley, CA, 2015), pp. 221–33.

18 Deniz Gevrek, 'Interracial Marriage, Migration, and Loving', *Review of Black Political Economy*, XLI (2014), pp. 25–6.

19 Beverly Guy-Sheftall and Johnnetta B. Cole, *Gender Talk: The Struggle for Women's Equality in African American Communities* (New York, 2003), p. 200.

20 Leith Mullings, *On Our Own Terms: Race, Class, and Gender in the Lives of African-American Women* (New York, 1997), p. 113.

21 Coretta M. Pittman, *Literacy in a Long Blues Note: Black Women's Literature and Music in the Late Nineteenth and Early Twentieth Centuries* (Jackson, MS, 2022), p. 152.

22 Ibid.

23 Zora Neale Hurston, *Jonah's Gourd Vine*, in *Zora Neale Hurston, Novels and Stories: Jonah's Gourd Vine/ Their Eyes Were Watching God/ Moses, Man of the Mountain/ Seraph on the Suwanee/ Selected Stories*, ed. Cheryl A. Wall (Washington, DC, 1995), p. 43.

24 Ibid.

25 Hurston, *Dust Tracks on a Road*, p. 53.

26 Ibid.

27 Hurston, *Jonah's Gourd Vine*, p. 4.

28 Ibid., pp. 6, 9.

29 Pittman, *Literacy in a Long Blues Note*, p. 153.

30 Ibid.

31 Wall, ed., *Zora Neale Hurston: Novels and Stories*, p. 77.

32 Ibid., p. 78.

33 Ibid.

34 Ibid., pp. 77, 79.

35 Pittman, *Literacy in a Long Blues Note*, p. 162.

36 Ibid., p. 85.

37 Hurston quoted ibid., p. 86.

38 Ibid.

39 Ibid.

40 Ibid., p. 87.

41 Ibid.

42 Ibid.

43 Ibid., p. 88.

44 Angela Davis, *Women, Race, and Class* (New York, 1981), p. 88.

45 Darlene Clark Hine, William C. Hine and Stanley Harrold, *The African-American Odyssey* (New York, 2017), p. 396.
46 Ibid.
47 Ibid.
48 Wall, ed., *Zora Neale Hurston: Novels and Stories*, p. 92.
49 Ibid., p. 93.
50 Ibid., p. 109.
51 Hurston, *Jonah's Gourd Vine*, p. 156.
52 Ibid., p. 155.
53 Ibid., p. 156.
54 Wall, ed., *Zora Neale Hurston: Novels and Stories*, p. 166.
55 Ibid., p. 168.
56 Alan Brown, '"De Beast" Within: The Role of Nature in Jonah's Gourd Vine', in *Zora in Florida*, ed. Steve Glassman and Kathryn Lee Seidel (Orlando, FL, 1991), p. 85.
57 Ibid.
58 Dan Ben Amos, Henry Glass and Elliot Orang, *Folkore Concepts: Histories and Critiques* (Bloomington, IN, 2020), p. 7.
59 bell hooks, *Yearning: Race, Gender, and Cultural Politics*, 2nd edn (New York, 2013), p. 137.
60 Ibid., pp. 137–8.
61 Marjorie Pryse, *Conjuring: Black Women, Fiction, and Literary Tradition* (Bloomington, IN, 1985), p. 11.
62 Ibid., pp. 11–12.
63 Robert Hemenway quoted ibid., p. 12.
64 Sophie Abramowitz, 'Trained and Taught This Song', *American Quarterly*, LXXII/4 (December 2020), p. 883.
65 Ibid., p. 881.
66 Ibid.
67 Ibid.
68 hooks, *Yearning*, p. 137.
69 Ibid.
70 Ibid.
71 Ibid.
72 Zora Neale Hurston, *Mules and Men* (Pittsburgh, PA, 1935), p. 1.
73 Ibid.
74 Ibid., p. 2.
75 Ibid.
76 Ibid.
77 Ibid.

78 Dana McKinnon Preu, 'A Literary Reading of *Mules and Men,* Part I', in *Zora in Florida,* ed. Glassman and Seidel, p. 60.

79 Ibid., pp. 60–61.

80 Beulah S. Hemmingway, 'Through the Prism of Africanity: A Preliminary Investigation of Zora Neale Hurston's *Mules and Men'*, in *Zora in Florida,* ed. Glassman and Seidel, p. 45.

81 Hurston, *Mules and Men,* p. 2.

82 Ibid.

83 Ibid., p. 88.

84 Washington, 'A Woman Half in Shadow', p. 9.

85 Ibid.

86 Ibid.

87 Zora Neale Hurston, *Moses, Man of the Mountain,* in *Zora Neale Hurston, Novels and Stories,* ed. Wall, p. 589.

88 Ibid., p. 588.

89 Ibid., p. 589.

90 Ibid.

91 Ibid.

92 Ibid.

93 Ibid.

94 Ibid., p. 591.

95 Ibid.

96 Ibid.

97 Ibid.

98 Ibid.

99 Robert J. Morris, 'Zora Neale Hurston's Ambitious Enigma: *Moses, Man of the Mountain'*, *CLA Journal,* XL/3 (March 1997), p. 305.

100 Ibid., p. 306.

101 Ibid.

102 Hurston, *Moses, Man of the Mountain,* p. 595.

103 Ibid., pp. 594–5.

104 Joshua Pederson, 'Letting Moses Go: Hurston and Reed, Disowning Exodus', *Twentieth Century Literature,* LVIII/3 (Fall 2012), p. 443.

105 Hemenway, *A Literary Biography,* p. 270.

106 Pederson, 'Letting Moses Go', p. 444.

107 Ibid.

108 Ibid.

109 Ibid.

110 Ibid.

111 Ibid., p. 443.

112 Houston A. Baker Jr, 'Intuiting Archives: Notes for a Post-Trauma Poetics', *African American Review*, XLIX/1 (Spring 2016), pp. 1–4.

113 Ibid., p. 2.

114 Ibid.

115 Cheryl A. Wall, *Worrying the Line: Black Women Writers, Lineage, and Literary Tradition* (Chapel Hill, NC, 2005), p. 308.

5 Stormy Weather

1 Stephen J. Glassman and Kathryn L. Seidel, eds, *Zora in Florida* (Gainesville, FL, 1991), p. xxii.

2 Henry Louis Gates Jr, 'Afterword', in *Dust Tracks on a Road: An Autobiography* (New York, 1996), p. 289.

3 Ibid.

4 Ibid., p. 288.

5 Ibid., p. 289.

6 Ibid.

7 Susan Bordo, *Twilight Zones: The Hidden Life of Cultural Images from Plato to O. J.* (Berkeley, CA, 1997), p. 181.

8 Ibid., p. 183.

9 Mae G. Henderson, 'Speaking in Tongues: Dialogics, Dialectics, and the Black Woman Writer's Literary Tradition', in *Changing Our Own Words: Essays on Criticism, Theory, and Writing by Black Women* (New Brunswick, NJ, 1991), p. 24.

10 Cheryl A. Wall, ed., *Zora Neale Hurston, Novels and Stories: Jonah's Gourd Vine/ Their Eyes Were Watching God/ Moses, Man of the Mountain/ Seraph on the Suwanee/ Selected Stories* (Washington, DC, 1995), p. 187.

11 Valerie Boyd, *Wrapped in Rainbows: The Life of Zora Neale Hurston* (New York, 2003), p. 301.

12 Ibid.

13 Ibid.

14 Ibid.

15 Wall, ed., *Zora Neale Hurston: Novels and Stories*, pp. 182–3.

16 Ibid., p. 325.

17 Ibid.

18 Patricia Hill Collins, *Black Feminist Thought: Knowledge, Consciousness, and the Politics of Empowerment* (Boston, MA, 1990), p. 25.

19 Miriam DeCosta-Willis, ed., *The Memphis Diary of Ida B. Wells: An Intimate Portrait of the Activist as a Young Woman* (Boston, MA, 1995), p. xii.
20 Ibid.
21 Ibid.
22 Pauli Murray, 'The Liberation of Black Women', in *Words of Fire: An Anthology of African American Feminist Thought*, ed. Beverly Guy-Sheftall (New York, 1995), p. 192.
23 Ibid., p. 195.
24 Ibid., p. 192.
25 Zora Neale Hurston, *Their Eyes Were Watching God* (Pittsburgh, PA, 1937), p. 193.
26 Ibid.
27 Ibid.
28 Ibid.
29 Ibid., pp. 192–3.
30 Ibid., p. 193.
31 Ibid.
32 Ibid.
33 Ibid.
34 Ibid.
35 Robert Hemenway, *Zora Neale Hurston: A Literary Biography* (Urbana, IL, 1977), pp. 248, 251.
36 Ibid., p. 248.
37 Alain Locke quoted ibid., p. 250.
38 Ibid., p. 249.
39 Ibid.
40 Ibid.
41 Ibid., p. 250.
42 Ibid.
43 Ibid.
44 Boyd, *Wrapped in Rainbows*, p. 320.
45 Ibid.
46 Ibid.
47 Ibid.
48 Ibid.
49 Ibid.
50 Barbara Speisman, 'Voodoo as Symbol in *Jonah's Gourd Vine*', in *Zora in Florida*, ed. Glassman and Seidel, p. 86; here, Speisman references Hurston's essay 'The Sanctified Church'.

51 Ibid.

52 Annette Trefzer, 'Possessing the Self: Caribbean Identities in Zora Neale Hurston's *Tell My Horse*', *African American Review*, xxxiv/2 (2000), p. 299.

53 Ibid.

54 Zora Neale Hurston, 'Tell My Horse', excerpted in *I Love Myself When I'm Laughing: A Zora Neale Hurston Reader*, ed. Alice Walker (New York, 2011), p. 128.

6 Featherbed Resistance

1 Cheryl A. Wall, ed., *Vine/ Their Eyes Were Watching God/ Moses, Man of the Mountain/ Seraph on the Suwanee/ Selected Stories* (Washington, DC, 1995), p. 1025.

2 Valerie Boyd, *Wrapped in Rainbows: The Life of Zora Neale Hurston* (New York, 2003), p. 347.

3 Ibid.

4 Hurston quoted ibid.

5 Zora Neale Hurston, *Dust Tracks on a Road* (New York, 1942), p. 276.

6 Ibid., p. 274.

7 Ibid., p. 276.

8 Carla Kaplan, *Zora Neale Hurston: A Life in Letters* (New York, 2002), p. 435.

9 Ibid., italics in original.

10 Ibid.

11 Ibid.

12 Kathleen Hassall, 'Text and Personality in Disguise and in the Open: Zora Neale Hurston's *Dust Tracks on a Road*', in *Zora in Florida*, ed. Steve Glassman and Kathryn Lee Seidel (Orlando, FL, 1991), p. 160.

13 Ibid.

14 Ibid.

15 Ibid.

16 Ibid.

17 Ibid., p. 171.

18 Wall, ed., *Zora Neale Hurston, Novels and Stories*, p. 1025.

19 Ibid.

20 Ibid.

21 Ibid.

22 As the novelist Tim O'Brien once intimated to me, 'Cheryl, I'm a writer. I lie a lot.'

23 Hurston, *Dust Tracks on a Road*, p. 214.

24 Toni Morrison, 'Nobel Lecture', 7 December 1993, www.nobelprize.org.

25 Wall, ed., *Zora Neale Hurston, Novels and Stories*, p. 1026.

26 Boyd, *Wrapped in Rainbows*, p. 377.

27 Ibid.

28 Hurston, *Dust Tracks on a Road*, p. 276.

29 bell hooks, *Ain't I a Woman? Black Women and Feminism* (Boston, MA, 1982), p. 15.

30 Ibid.

31 Wall, ed., *Zora Neale Hurston: Novels and Stories*, p. 632.

32 Chris Roark, 'Hurston's Shakespeare: "Something like a King Only Bigger and Better"', *CLA Journal*, LX/2 (December 1996), pp. 205–13, p. 205.

33 Adrienne Akins, '"Just like Mister Jim": Class Transformation from Cracker to Aristocrat in Hurston's *Seraph on the Suwanee*', *Mississippi Quarterly*, LXIII/2 (Winter 2010), pp. 31–43, p. 33.

34 Boyd, *Wrapped in Rainbows*, p. 391.

35 Ibid.

36 Ibid.

37 Akins, '"Just like Mister Jim"', p. 32.

7 The Dulling Final Years

1 Zora Neal Hurston, letter to Carl Sandburg, 12 June 1950, in *Zora Neale Hurston: A Life in Letters*, ed. Carla Kaplan (New York, 2002), p. 628.

2 Ibid.

3 Zora Neale Hurston, letter to Sara Lee Creech, 29 June 1950, in *A Life in Letters*, ed. Kaplan, p. 630.

4 Alice Walker, ed., *I Love Myself When I Am Laughing: A Zora Neale Hurston Reader* (New York, 1979), p. xv.

5 Ibid.

6 Ibid.

7 Ibid.

8 Ibid.

9 Ibid., p. xvi.

10 Valerie Boyd, *Wrapped in Rainbows: The Life of Zora Neale Hurston* (New York, 2003), p. 408.

11 Cheryl A. Wall, ed., *Zora Neale Hurston, Novels and Stories: Jonah's Gourd Vine/ Their Eyes Were Watching God/ Moses, Man of the Mountain/ Seraph on the Suwanee/ Selected Stories* (Washington, DC, 1995), p. 1029.

12 Boyd, *Wrapped in Rainbows*, p. 407.

13 Ibid.

14 Ibid.

15 Ibid., p. 408.

16 Ibid.

17 Wall, *Zora Neale Hurston: Novels and Stories*, p. 1030.

18 Ibid.

19 Ibid.

20 Ibid.

21 Ibid.

22 Ibid.

23 Ibid.

24 Ibid.

25 Ibid., p. 1031.

26 Ibid.

27 Ibid.

28 Ibid.

29 Kaplan, ed., *A Life in Letters*, p. 614.

30 Ibid.

31 Ibid.

32 Robert Hemenway, *Zora Neale Hurston: A Literary Biography* (Urbana, IL, 1977), p. 346.

33 Wall, ed., *Zora Neale Hurston: Novels and Stories*, p. 1032 and p. 346.

34 Kaplan, ed., *A Life in Letters*, p. 615.

35 Ibid.

36 Hemenway, *A Literary Biography*, p. 346.

37 Ibid.

38 Ibid.

39 Ibid., p. 347.

40 Ibid.

41 Ibid.

42 Ibid., p. 1030.

43 Mary Helen Washington, 'Zora Neale Hurston: A Woman Half in Shadow', in *I Love Myself When I Am Laughing*, ed. Walker, p. 17.

44 Quoted in Hemenway, *A Literary Biography*, p. 348.

45 Boyd, *Wrapped in Rainbows*, p. 432.

46 Ibid.

47 Ibid.

48 According to Anna Lillios, 'Excursions into Zora Neale Hurston's Eatonville', in *Zora in Florida*, ed. Steve Glassman and Kathryn Lee Seidel (Orlando, FL, 1991), p. 13.

49 Boyd, *Wrapped in Rainbows*, p. 432.

50 By the *Fort Pierce Chronicle*, quoted ibid.

51 Ibid.

52 Quoted in Hemenway, *A Literary Biography*, p. 348.

Epilogue: 'I'm Not Done Yet'

1 Tressie McMillan-Cottom, *Thick: And Other Essays* (New York, 2019), p. 207.

2 Ibid., p. 94.

3 A line from and the title of Hurston's short story 'Drenched in Light' of 1924.

4 Zora Neale Hurston, *Dust Tracks on a Road* (New York, 1942), p. 262.

5 Valerie Boyd, *Wrapped in Rainbows: The Life of Zora Neale Hurston* (New York, 2003), p. 68.

6 Ibid.

7 Carla Kaplan, ed., *Zora Neale Hurston: A Life in Letters* (New York, 2002), p. 39.

8 Ibid.

9 Alice Walker, *Anything We Love Can Be Saved* (New York, 1998), p. 67.

10 Alice Walker, *In Search of Our Mothers' Gardens* (New York, 1983), p. xi.

11 Hurston, *Dust Tracks on a Road*, p. 68.

12 Alice Walker, ed., *I Love Myself When I Am Laughing: A Zora Neale Hurston Reader* (New York, 1979), p. 153.

13 Hurston, *Dust Tracks on a Road*, p. 207.

14 Henry Louis Gates Jr, 'Afterword', in Zora Neale Hurston, *Mules and Men* (New York, 2008), p. 290.

15 Ibid., p. 288.

16 Ibid., p. 291.

17 Ibid., pp. 287–8.

18 Ibid., p. 288.

19 Ibid.

20 Quoted in Kaplan, ed., *A Life in Letters*, p. 5.

Select Bibliography

Works by Zora Neale Hurston
Jonah's Gourd Vine (Philadelphia, PA, 1934)
Mules and Men (Philadelphia, PA, 1935)
Their Eyes Were Watching God (New York, 1937)
Tell My Horse (Philadelphia, PA, 1938)
Moses, Man of the Mountain (Philadelphia, PA, 1939)
Seraph on the Suwanee (New York, 1948)
Zora Neale Hurston, Novels and Stories: Jonah's Gourd Vine/ Their Eyes Were Watching God/ Moses, Man of the Mountain/ Seraph on the Suwanee/ Selected Stories, ed. Cheryl A. Wall (Washington, DC, 1995)
Zora Neale Hurston: The Complete Stories (New York, 2008)
Barracoon: The Story of the Last 'Black Cargo' (New York, 2018)
Hitting a Straight Lick with a Crooked Stick: Stories from the Harlem Renaissance (New York, 2020)
You Don't Know Us Negroes, and Other Essays (New York, 2022)
I Love Myself When I Am Laughing (New York, 2011)

On Zora Neale Hurston
Boyd, Valerie, *Wrapped in Rainbows: The Life of Zora Neale Hurston* (New York, 2003)
Bracks, Lean'tin L., and Jessie Carney Smith, eds, *Black Women of the Harlem Renaissance Era* (Lanham, MD, 2014)
Hemenway, Robert, *Zora Neale Hurston: A Literary Biography* (Urbana, IL, 1977)
Howard, Lillie P., *Zora Neale Hurston* (Woodbridge, CT, 1980)
Jones, Sharon L., ed., *Critical Insights: Zora Neale Hurston* (Hackensack, NJ, 2013)

Kaplan, Carla, ed., *Zora Neale Hurston: A Life in Letters* (New York, 2003)

Perry, Imani, *South to America: A Journey below the Mason-Dixon to Understand the Soul of a Nation* (New York, 2023)

Taylor, Yuval, *Zora and Langston: A Story of Friendship and Betrayal* (New York, 2019)

Wall, Cheryl A., *Women of the Harlem Renaissance* (Bloomington, IN, 1995)

Articles and Essays

Abramowitz, Sophie, 'Trained and Taught This Song by Zora Hurston', *American Quarterly*, LXXII/4 (December 2020), pp. 881–908

Akins, Adrienne, '"Just like Mister Jim": Class Transformation from Cracker to Aristocrat in Hurston's *Seraph on the Suwanee*', *Mississippi Quarterly*, LXIII/1 (Winter 2010), pp. 31–43

Albano, Alessandra, 'Nature and Black Femininity in Hurston's *Their Eyes Were Watching God* and *Tell My Horse*', *Journal of African American Studies*, XXIV/1 (March 2020), pp. 23–36

Baker, Houston A. Jr, 'Intuiting Archives: Notes for a Post-Trauma Poetics', *African American Review*, XLIX/1 (Spring 2016), pp. 1–4

Binggeli, Elizabeth, 'The Unadapted: Warner Bros. Reads Zora Neale Hurston', *Cinema Journal*, XLVIII/3 (Spring 2009), pp. 1–15

Brown, Adrienne, 'Hard Romping: Zora Neale Hurston, White Women, and the Right to Play', *Twentieth Century Literature*, LXIV/3 (September 2018), pp. 295–316

Carter, Catherine, 'The God in the Snake, the Devil in the Phallus: Biblical Revision and Radical Conservatism in Hurston's "Sweat"', *Mississippi Quarterly*, LXVII/4 (2014), pp. 605–20

Delbanco, Andrew, 'The Political Incorrectness of Zora Neale Hurston', *Journal of Blacks in Higher Education*, XVIII (Winter 1997–8), pp. 103–8

Diamond, Elin, 'Folk Modernism: Zora Neale Hurston's Gestural Drama', *Modern Drama*, LVIII/1 (2015), pp. 112–34

Dutton, Wendy, 'The Problem of Invisibility: Voodoo and Zora Neale Hurston', *Frontiers: A Journal of Women Studies*, XIII/2 (1993), pp. 131–52

Edwards, Erica R., 'Moses, Monster of the Mountain: Gendered Violence in Black Leadership's Gothic Tale', *Callaloo*, XXXI/4 (Fall 2008), pp. 1084–102

Harney, Daniel, 'Scholarship and the Modernist Public: Zora Neale Hurston and the Limitations of Art and Disciplinary Anthropology', *Modernism/Modernity*, XXII/3 (September 2015), pp. 471–92

Kam, Tanya Y., 'Velvet Coats and Manicured Nails: The Body Speaks Resistance in *Dust Tracks on a Road*', *Southern Literary Journal*, XLII/1 (Fall 2009), pp. 73–87

Morrell, Sascha, '"There Is No Female Word for Busha in These Parts": Zora Neale Hurston, Katherine Dunham and Women's Experience in 1930s Haiti and Jamaica', *Australian Humanities Review*, LXIV (May 2019)

Pederson, Joshua, 'Letting Moses Go: Hurston and Reed, Disowning Exodus', *Twentieth Century Literature*, LVIII/3 (Fall 2012), pp. 439–61

Schmidt, Amy, 'Horses Chomping at the Global Bit: Ideology, Systemic Injustice, and Resistance in Zora Neale Hurston's *Tell My Horse*', *Southern Literary Journal*, XLVI/2 (Spring 2014), pp. 173–92

Seymour, Gene, 'Sharpening Her Oyster Knife', *Bookforum*, XXIX/1 (March–May 2022)

Stewart, Lindsey, '"Tell 'Em Boy Bye": Zora Neale Hurston and the Importance of Refusal', *Signs: Journal of Women in Culture and Society*, XLVI/1 (Autumn 2020), pp. 57–77

Select Filmography

Martin, Darnell, dir., *Their Eyes Were Watching God* (Harpo Films, 2005)

Pollard, Sam, dir., *Zora Neale Hurston: Jump at the Sun* (Bay Bottom News, 2008)

Strain, Tracy Heather, dir., *Zora Neale Hurston: Claiming a Space* (PBS, 2023)

Acknowledgements

The author would like to thank Western Kentucky University for her sabbatical semester – time that was devoted to the development of this book – for a course release to complete editing and for funding to undertake research in the Zora Neale Hurston Papers at the University of Florida, Gainesville, and the Valerie Boyd Papers at Emory University in Atlanta, Georgia. The author would also like to thank her editors, Vivian Constantinopoulos and Amy Salter, at Reaktion Books. Finally, the author would like to thank Alice Walker, for pointing the way, and Zora Neale Hurston, for laying down the road and leaving tracks.

Photo Acknowledgements

The author and publishers wish to express their thanks to the below sources of illustrative material and/or permission to reproduce it:

George A. Smathers Libraries, University of Florida, Zora Neale Hurston Papers, Gainesville, FL: pp. 6, 9, 10, 11, 22, 23, 25, 28, 39, 55, 56, 64, 65 (above), 74, 75, 78, 112, 125, 132, 136, 142, 144; Library of Congress Prints and Photographs Division, Washington, DC: pp. 30, 65 (below).